PUB WALKS
IN
Lancashire

THIRTY CIRCULAR WALKS
AROUND LANCASHIRE INNS

Alan Shepley

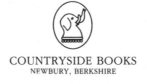

COUNTRYSIDE BOOKS
NEWBURY, BERKSHIRE

COUNTRYSIDE BOOKS
3 Catherine Road
Newbury, Berkshire

ISBN 1 85306 296 0

06163175

Designed by Mon Mohan
Cover illustration by Colin Doggett
Photographs and maps by the author

Produced through MRM Associates Ltd., Reading
Typeset by Paragon Typesetters, Queensferry, Clwyd
Printed in England

Contents

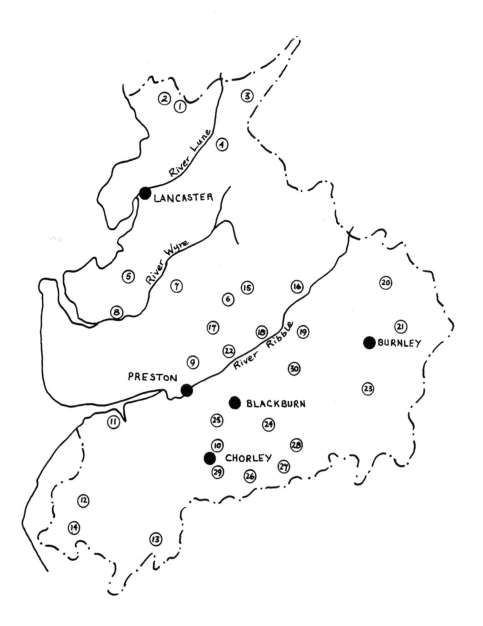

Area map showing locations of the walks.

Publisher's Note

We hope that you obtain considerable enjoyment from this book; great care has been taken in its preparation. However, changes of landlord and actual closures are sadly not uncommon. Likewise, although at the time of publication all routes followed public rights of way or well-established permitted paths, diversion orders can be made and permissions withdrawn.

We cannot accept responsibility for any inaccuracies, but we are anxious that all details covering both pubs and walks are kept up to date, and would therefore welcome information from readers which would be relevant to future editions.

Introduction

Despite all the changes wrought over recent years, the English pub remains a unique part of the scene and is justifiably famed far and wide and, despite the increasing spread of car ownership (or perhaps because of it?), the English on the whole still have a happy habit of walking about their countryside for their leisure and pleasure. What then could make for greater enjoyment than to combine the two and to link a little gentle exercise with a drink or food (or drink and food) at a good pub either before or after – or both?

The pubs of Lancashire give ground to no other part of the country in their quality and it has been no easy task to choose just 30 from hundreds. Many of the pubs in the county are clearly urban in location and I leave the reader to make his or her own choice and sample of these. Country ones, however, tend to be very much part of the local landscape and are often an important feature of the place today just as much as they were in days gone by when perhaps more trade was conducted in a bar over a pint of good ale than anywhere else.

As a deliberate policy, I have endeavoured to seek out walks in each of the present districts of the county created in the reorganisation of 1974. Regrettably this means that the area north of Morecambe Bay has had to be excluded, as has the south-west coast, but we have gained the beauties of Bowland and the edges of Craven. Even when the walks were well known to me I have re-walked each of them during the preparation of this book to ensure that the route details given are as accurate as practicable. Please keep in mind, however, that the countryside is a continually changing pattern and is a work place as well as an attractive landscape. As a consequence, paths do change from time to time quite legally, as well as illegally! It is always worthwhile chatting with local people, who are much more likely to be helpful than otherwise, and who will know of changes and problems, perhaps adding snippets of fact and story which you will not otherwise glean. Carrying the 1:50 000 Ordnance Survey Landranger map is a sensible precaution to help determine the correct route when it is unclearly marked on the ground, and the appropriate sheet number is indicated for each walk. The presumption is that you will probably want a half-day walk and the distances have been mostly chosen with this in mind. How long it actually takes will obviously depend on how used you are to walking, what the weather is like, and who your companions are; distance can only be taken as a rough guide to time. There is no reason why one walk cannot be extended using the map or a second undertaken on the same day.

Lancashire has its share of rainy days so always ensure you are prepared for this. The result is often wet and muddy walking in places along country routes and it is wise to wear stout shoes or boots; I have tried to indicate where I think it likely these will be needed. None of the climbs are particularly high and I do not expect you will have any doubt about the route, even in poor visibility.

Licensees and landlords are as variable as landscapes and will have their own approach to your taking your own food, in which parts of the pub children may be allowed, whether or not you may bring your dog inside, leave your car in their car park while you go for a walk, and so on. Where practicable, the views of the landlord on such matters are indicated in each description. Where there is no comment you may assume the answer will be negative; do remember, however, that in such cases you may not meet the same person that I did and a polite enquiry beforehand is well worth it.

All of the suggested pubs serve food as well as drink but times for both will vary from place to place, almost certainly they will vary through the year, and may be altered at short notice. Some places are extemely popular and booking ahead is advisable if you want more than a bar meal. Longer opening hours and the likelihood that tea or coffee and bar snacks will be available throughout the day now make for much more flexibility in planning a day out including a walk. Should you need to make enquiries telephone numbers have been included. The facilities that each pub offers vary a great deal and I have tried to include a range of pubs on this basis. Some landlords endeavour to attract custom with an amazing variety of offerings, some choose to attract by specialising in some way – perhaps just by being plain and simple in what they see as the old style. Either way there is plenty of choice for everyone.

My own joy in walking these ways has been the feeling of continuity between past and present which accompanies every step. You too will surely enjoy your Lancashire walking. Remember, always, the Country Code, the true purpose of which, after all, is to pass on our heritage improved, not impaired.

Lastly, I have to thank all who have helped in the preparation of this book, including those landlords who willingly gave me information about their pubs. This also includes those friends who shared their enthusiasms for particular pubs and places and the many who have gone before and written about this lovely countryside. I thank them one and all: cheers!

Alan Shepley
spring 1994

Tewitfield
The Longlands Hotel

1

Tewitfield (the field of the lapwings) was once a busy industrial basin with nearby cinder ovens, the product of which was a flux for iron smelting. Coal from small pits around Farleton, and lime from numerous kilns in the area, were transported on the canal. Today the steady roar of the traffic on the M6 emphasises how such developments have moved on.

Where the north road from Lancaster branches in two and meets the canal is an obvious place for a coaching inn to have been established and the imposing late-Georgian façade of the Longlands Hotel stands out to the passer-by on the modern M6 which parallels the old routes. The whole building has been recently refurbished; the east wing retains an old world atmosphere with low beams, a cheerful open fire and a well-used dartboard which suggests strong local trade, whilst the west wing has an airy modern bar room and restaurant. The management aims for a good-quality straightforward service. As this is a freehouse a wide variety of bottled beers and drinks are stocked. The landlords also carry Worthington and Bass bitter in barrel and Blackthorn cider in keg in response to a good trade from leisure craft on the canal, large local caravan sites, and the continuing passing trade. Normal licensing hours are 11 am to 11 pm and 12 noon to 3 pm on Sundays with an evening supper licence. Substantial bar snacks are available from noon every day and the restaurant is open between noon and 2 pm on Mondays and to 9.30 pm other days of the week (on Monday evenings six- or seven-piece bands perform in the restaurant). The à la carte menu has a small but increasing range, including a vegetarian dish, and a special dish is available each day. Children are welcome in the reception area, restaurant and beer garden and they have their own garden play area. Owners are requested to check at the bar before bringing dogs into the hotel. Accommodation is available, but it is wise to check availability and current prices by a prior telephone call.

Telephone: 0524 781256.

How to get there: Bear right for ½ mile along the A6070, signed for Burton, from the A6 ½ mile north of the M6 junction 35 for Carnforth.

Parking: The hotel has a large adjacent car park which customers are welcome to use by arrangement during their walk. As an alternative, there is roadside parking either side of the bridge beside Tewitfield Methodist church (GR 521734).

Length of the walk: 3 miles. Map: OS Landranger 97 Kendal and Morecambe (GR 520736).

This is easy and pleasant walking; the distance indicated is simply that of the longest possible loop – a glance at the sketch map will indicate several other shorter possibilities which will enable you to adjust your time or to avoid muddy fields after heavy rain. The walk links the present end of the navigable stretch of the Lancaster canal with the attractive village of Borwick (the place where barley was grown), founded before the Normans came, and its Elizabethan Hall.

The Walk
Cross the A6070 in front of the hotel and take the signed bridleway a few yards to the right and walk the length of the buildings of Greenlands farm to join the stoned track which leads up the low hill. In approximately 200 yards the track flattens and you will find a pair of metal field gates next to each other on the left at about the point where a bridge over the canal comes into sight. Go through the second of the gates and drop between hedges towards the canal and motorway and bend right past a ruined shed to the bridge. Cross and bear left down the towpath beside what was once the famous flight of Tewitfield Locks, completed in 1818; there were eight of them with a total ascent of 76 ft and they were built wide enough to take sea-

9

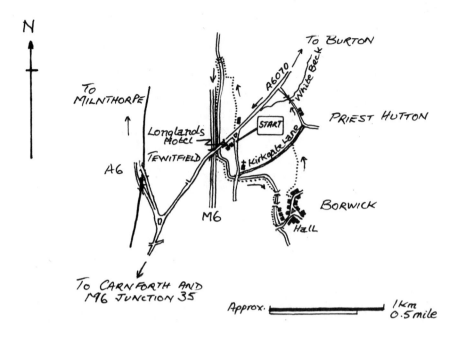

N

To BURTON

To MILNTHORPE

A6070 →

White Beck

PRIEST HUTTON

Longlands Hotel

START

Kirkoalk Lane

A6

TEWITFIELD

BORWICK

M6

Hall

To CARNFORTH AND M6 JUNCTION 35

Approx. ⊢━━━━━━━━━━━┥ 1 km / 0.5 mile

going vessels up to Kendal. The gates have now been replaced by weirs. The embankment which carries the A6070 bridge over the M6 resulted in the destruction of a skew bridge over the canal, which is now culverted underneath, and the stopping of navigation except for canoes. It is possible to use the steps to go up and over the motorway and view the depression in the field to the west which is all that is left of an earlier line for the canal. The towpath is almost a walkway beside the M6 under the bridge and then swings up to Tewitfield basin with moorings, toilets, picnic site, children's play area and information board.

The canal bends east and a second picnic site is soon reached beside bridge 138. Across to the right the wooded top of the limestone crag of Warton stands out, easily distinguishable as the commanding site of an Iron Age fort. The village at its foot was the later centre of a Norman manor. Through the bridge and over on the other side of the canal stands a Wesleyan Methodist church of 1886 which is still in use. On the far side you pass an old milestone in the hedge (Kendal 12 miles/Lancaster 15 miles) and beyond a wooded bank over the canal you reach bridge 137. The first buildings of Borwick then come into view above Sander's Bridge (136) and just beyond it the gardens of several modern bungalows run down to the canal. At bridge 135 climb up to the right and then back across the canal to walk up the lane into Borwick village beside the converted barn and stable buildings of Borwick Hall (now a centre for Youth Service training). The Hall is best seen from the village green. In the centre of the mass of buildings is the original 14th century pele tower around which Robert Bindloss, a Kendal clothier, erected his imposing mansion in the 1590s; viewing is only occasionally possible. The stones amongst the trees on the green itself are all that remain of a chapel. Many of the houses of the village are attractively built in the local limestone. All round Borwick the landscape is formed of low hills of material left behind by the retreating ice 10,000 years ago, and which now form rich grazing.

Turn round to the left past the parish noticeboard to a footpath sign beside Corner Cottage and go left for 50 yards along a concreted track. At this point the track runs half-left towards the canal again but the path goes right at the field gate, along the farm buildings, to a stile hidden behind a modern slurry tank, and into the field beyond. Go left over the stile in the fence past the first hedge on the left and bear diagonally right up the field to a gate in the hedge with a broken stile on the right of it. The view is of massive, glacially deposited smooth-topped mounds scattered across the valley with the limestone crags of Hutton Roof (across the boundary in Cumbria) beyond. Walk ahead through a stone squeeze stile and between hedges to a footpath sign at the unmade Kirkgate Lane (the Methodist church is along to your left now). Turn right and drop down to the metalled lane at the edge of the village of Priest Hutton.

Complete the circuit by walking left along the lane, past a couple of pre-war detached houses on the right and over White Beck bridge, to the A6070 with the scattered parkland trees of Buckstone House on the hill immediately ahead. At the T-junction cross the road and walk left along the grass verge to return to the Longlands Hotel past a small nursery garden on the left.

Yealand Conyers
The New Inn

The string of villages along the old road to the east of a low limestone ridge on the west of the valley of the river Keer runs north from Warton, through Yealand Redmayne and Yealand Conyers, to Yealand Storrs like the shells of a necklace made by a child. It is this ridge which gives the Yealands (high land) their first name with Conyers and Redmayne being family names and Storrs indicating 'scrubland' – still apt today. The villages grow out of the rock of the hillside and the New Inn with its adjacent barn, beside a double bend in the street, fits in superbly.

There are few New Inns which are new, and this is no exception. At some time over 400 years ago it replaced a predecessor and was 'new' for but a short while. Today it blends in with the long street of the village and only the signs draw attention to what appears outwardly to be a largish house similar to several others. The licensee is keen to maintain this feeling of homeliness and the inner appearance of the bar, lounge and dining areas has been kept cosy, with a feeling of warmth even when the open fire is not ablaze. Drinking times are 12 noon to 3 pm and 7 pm to 10.30 pm throughout the week with ample opportunity to sample the real ales of Hartleys (formerly of

Ulverston) and Robinson's breweries. There is a wide range of bar snacks available, ranging from simple soup and ham to rump steak and deep-fried Camembert, and vegetarian choices. The restaurant offerings include a starter of herrings in madeira sauce and medallions of pork cooked with orange segments and fresh root ginger, flamed in brandy and finished with cream. The aim is to provide high-quality meats and fish in fascinating complementary sauces. The main problem is dragging yourself away from the table once you have got there. Weekday times for food are 11.30 am to 1.45 pm and 6 pm to 9 pm with Sundays 12 noon to 3 pm and 7 pm to 8.45 pm. Booking is advisable, especially at weekends. Children are welcome in the beer garden, but the premises are not suitable for dogs.

Telephone: 0524 732928.

How to get there: Follow the signs for Yealand Conyers from the A6 about 2 miles north of Junction 35 of the M6. Several lanes lead to the road linking Warton to Leighton Moss RSPB bird reserve; the New Inn is about ½ mile north of the lane signed to Leighton Hall.

Parking: The car park beside the inn is not extensive and may prove too retricted at weekends; permission should be sought to leave your car there whilst walking. Alternatives exist at approximately the halfway point of the walk (GR 493761) beside the road just north of Yealand Storrs (which brings the advantage of walking along the road past Yealand Hall and its resident cock on the midden!) or beside the picnic site below your path between Yealand Storrs and Yealand Redmayne (GR 498761).

Length of the walk: 3½ miles. Map: OS Landranger 97 Kendal and Morecambe (GR 504748).

At most seasons you will be unlucky if you do not meet roe deer in the woods or small groups of fallow deer on the mosses. The woodlands are mainly former coppices of broadleaved trees which have, in part, been converted to forest of individual large trees. In this area the native small-leaved lime is still common and some of the coppice stools have been cut over for more than a thousand years. In contrast, the drainage of the mosses is much more recent, having been mainly undertaken in the last 150 years.

This is an easy walk apart from a short rocky section near Deepdale Pond that can be avoided by following the alternative path shown on the sketch map which cuts directly through the wood and shortens the distance by about ½ mile. The circuit contrasts the wooded limestone ridge of Cringlebarrow with the mosslands and fields to the east of the Yealands.

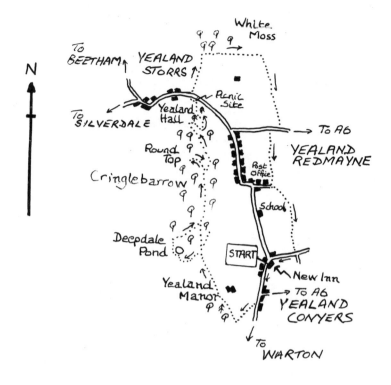

N

Approx |━━━━━━━━━━| 1 km
0.5 mile

The Walk

Leave the inn and walk up the lane a short way to steps and an iron railing on the right across the road from The Old Post House. The path climbs gently between the parkland trees of Yealand Manor, built in classical style in 1805. Cross the driveway and pass some young copper beeches and an old iron lift-pump to the left to reach the edge of the wood. Make your way half-right under a sweet chestnut tree and rise slightly to cross through the wood immediately behind the manor buildings. At the far end you will exit into a long field with a clear track running through it. Follow this to a gate at the far end in a narrow corner – ignore the gate on the right. The short route is through the gate and bear left off the track along a path after 50 yards. Otherwise, turn left over a stile within the field on the left, and scramble up the natural steps of limestone pavement and follow the path steeply down amongst limestone boulders with fine growths of

14

hart's tongue fern. Here, in an almost circular hollow of the hill, lies the still and murky water of Deepdale Pond with the eerie spectres of twisted alder and willow giving a rather forbidding aspect to both the heat of a shaded July afternoon or the fading light of winter. Walk clockwise round the pond through tall bracken and wild raspberries. Climb out the far side to a sign on a track and turn right.

The track rises and crosses an old wall into more open woodland on top of Cringlebarrow and is reunited with the through route along which you should now turn to the left. Keep to the east of the crest beside small cliffs for a while and then drop down to the right. At a post marked with a footpath arrow pointing left, it is worth the diversion to scramble up a zigzag through a glade of yews to Round Top where a magnificent panorama across the Kent estuary to the Lakeland fells opens up before you; do not continue but retrace your steps to the main path. Continue as the path narrows over blocks of limestone pavement until you reach a T-junction and turn right and climb gently up the track to pass a small pond on the left and reach a second T-junction. Turn left and pass through an iron gate within 50 yards and walk along between fences along an avenue of Scots pines in a plantation of young spruce. At the end of the limestone wall on your right walk straight ahead and descend behind a tiny picnic site to reach the lane to Yealand Storrs.

Go through the gate directly across and walk diagonally right down the field to the wicket gate in the right-hand corner following the bridleway. As you descend the view widens to stretch from The Helm, behind Kendal, through Farleton Knott ahead, round to the fells behind Lancaster to the south. Ignore the angle of the arrow on the wicket and go directly ahead across the field to a second wicket gate and then turn right along the edge of woodland interspersed with long fields reclaimed from the peat of White Moss. The drains grow massive watercress and your step acquires bounce on the springy peat.

At an enclosure on the left with several huts (where you will probably be eyed askance by goats) the track becomes surfaced and you should turn right through the gate in 50 yards. Walk between hedges of roses and elder, thick with meadowsweet in season, with the roofs of Yealand Redmayne appearing on the slope to the right. At the metalled road turn right for 50 yards and then go left through the squeeze stile. The path follows through the fields, and a series of squeeze stiles, parallel to the village to join a track at a right-angled corner. Go straight ahead to the bottom of Well Lane; to the right is the village post office and store. Immediately on your left is the well with an iron lift-pump over a large limestone trough. Walk past it and cross to a stile on the right and a sign for Rose Acre Lane. A further series of squeeze stiles takes you through the fields behind the

National School (built in 1841) and the village hall; the section where the path jigs right through a gate to run between overgrown hedges can be muddy after rain. You emerge on to the lane beside a house named Blencathra with the village church of St John (1838) ahead – another of the many now, sadly, kept locked because of vandalism. Turn right and walk up to the inn. On the way admire the view east-south-east towards the Yorkshire Dales and Ingleborough.

If you have the time and the inclination to extend your visit to the area, it is worth looking at the Friends Meeting House, which was originally constructed as early as 1692, beside the turn for Leighton Hall, and visiting the Hall itself. It is open between May and September and contains a fine collection of furniture, paintings, silver and clocks. Afternoon displays of free-flying birds of prey are given in the grounds. For enquiries telephone 0524 734474.

Cowan Bridge
Whoop Hall

Whoop Hall (pronounced without the 'w' – the name is probably a corruption of 'Upper Hall') has served travellers along the main road north from west Yorkshire and east Lancashire for over 350 years; when Wordsworth was a lad this was *the* route, for it avoided the sands of Morecambe Bay. In former times the local foxhounds met here and, for a while, the inn was actually owned by the trustees for the poor of Gargrave, near Skipton. Sensible conversions of outbuildings in recent years have extended the facilities considerably. Overnight accommodation is, perhaps, in the upper-middle range of cost and includes accommodation for the disabled.

This is one of the few pubs where even those on a day's outing can start with breakfast if they wish. In addition to sandwiches and the specials of the day, the Buttery offers an all-day menu including the usual choices plus things like kebabs and crespelli (try 'em and see!) with a particularly good vegetarian choice. The Gallery Restaurant (from 6 pm to 10 pm) is for the serious eater and ranges through Cajun chicken to pork and apple en croûte, beef Wellington and a greater range of fish than is usual. Theakston and Boddingtons beers are carried, together with Murphy's stout and a guest beer; draught cider and no less than five lagers are available. Monday to Saturday you can indulge your taste between 11 am and 11 pm, whilst the Sunday hours are 12 noon to 3 pm and 7 pm to 10.30 pm. Families are well catered for. There are extended outside areas with patio and lawns and the bottom bar is set aside for family use. The policy is to reserve a no-smoking area. Guide dogs are welcome.

Telephone: 052 42 72154.

How to get there: The Whoop Hall stands beside the A65 about 1 mile on the Kirkby Lonsdale side of Cowan Bridge.

Parking: The car parking area is exceptionally generous. An alternative, avoiding the walk along the spur route to and from the pub, is outside the village hall just up the lane behind Cowan Bridge post office and store.

Length of the walk: 6 miles, reduced to 4½ if the spur is not used. Map: OS Landranger 97 Kendal and Morecambe (GR 624773).

The walk is fairly flat throughout, initially following the Leck beck on its course towards the river Lune and then swinging round over minor rises, which give good views of the higher fells, and returns via Cowan Bridge itself. The notice on the footbridge at Overtown indicates the force the Leck beck can exert when in flood and at least one similar bridge just above Cowan Bridge has disappeared in recent years. Downstream, on the northern side of Burrow bridge, is the site of a Roman fort (which might, possibly, have been called Calacum) but there is little to see except bumps in the field in front of the 18th century Burrow Hall. At the northern end of the bridge at Cowan Bridge is the building in which the Brontë sisters went to school, as a stone plaque let into the wall records. On the upstream side of the bridge a small viaduct carried the 'Little' Northwestern Railway across the beck and on the downstream side the remains of a fish ladder can be seen, hard below the wall.

The Walk

A spur connects the main route to the pub. Take this by following the footpath sign directly to the stile out of the southern corner of the car park and bear half-right past the fence corner. Immediately you will have a view of the fells round from Gragareth above the upper Leck valley, east to Ingleborough and south to the Hindburn valley and Goodber Common in Bowland. Drop a little and cross the small caravan site at New House to a footbridge; cross this and turn right. Pass through the broken gate with a plantation to the right and negotiate the Eller beck on stepping stones. A double stile across the

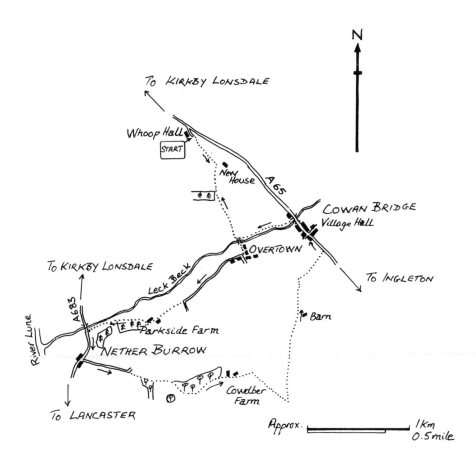

N

To KIRKBY LONSDALE

Whoop Hall

START

New House

A65

COWAN BRIDGE
Village Hall

OVERTOWN

To KIRKBY LONSDALE

Leck Beck

A683

To INGLETON

River Lune

Barn

Parkside Farm

NETHER BURROW

Cowdber Farm

To LANCASTER

Approx. ⌐────────┐ 1Km
0.5mile

field leads through to a cattle grid on an access track.

Turn left and right across the Leck beck into the hamlet of Overtown and walk past the cottages to reach a metalled lane beside the parish noticeboard. Turn right along the high-hedged lane, past masses of trailing goosegrass in season, to a gate at a right-angled bend. Continue ahead through the gate and under an oak tree to an old track which leads direct into the yard of Parkside farm. At the far end go right into the field between the large barn and the plantation and follow first the wall and then the river bank through to the stile by Burrow bridge; the narrow part of the field may well be churned up by cattle. Walk left along the verge of the A683 round the bend to the Highwayman pub and the cottages of Nether Burrow and go left again up Woodmans Lane. The view to the right is down the valley of the

19

Lune towards Hornby woods. At the right-angled bend continue directly ahead on the track (there is no sign) past a new house on your right.

Keasber Hill, with its circular oak wood, is on the rise to your right and the track eventually reaches Cowdber farm at its newly renovated barn. Walk across the front to a gate in the left-hand corner of the field; go half-right to a gate and stile on the far side of which is a cress-filled ditch. Stride across this to use the gate beside it, then aim just left of the farm roofs which are now in sight to cross two stiles over wire fences and reach a gate in the hedge a little right of the short piece of wall. Cross diagonally right to a second gate and then go hard left, almost back on yourself, up the field on the faint line of an old track to an unusually small gate by the angle of the hedge on the brow. The view opens up again all round and the crags of Hutton Roof should now be clear to your left. These open grazings are home to curlew, partridge and hare and you may see heron on their way to and from the river.

The path drops slowly down now, across two stone walls, and then slightly right towards the barn at Harlen Well. Take the track beyond the barn between walls and hedges, which are overgrown in summer, to a stile on the right on the near side of the fourth field boundary on the right. The line is direct through to the A65 now opposite Lakeland Woollens (if you pick the right day you will have a chance to visit the annual sale). Turn left along the verge to the village, pass the Methodist church, and cross the bridge to the Old School House, then take the path to the left along the northern bank of the river. This passes under a tunnel of blackthorn and can be a little difficult further on in high summer amongst a thick and tasty growth of wild raspberries. At the cattle grid turn right along the spur back to Whoop Hall.

4 Wray
The New Inn

The village of Wray lies at the confluence of the river Roeburn with the Hindburn and is as hidden away now as it was when our Norse ancestors first gave it name. Much of the present village is built in local sandstone, which has a greater variety of hue than many, and there are several late 19th century (and even one or two modern) buildings tastefully blended in. Holy Trinity church was built in 1840. The school building was restored in 1885 but a stone recalls that it was the gift of Captain Richard Pooley who gave £200 'for ever'; a resident of one of the nearby houses told me that the money still supports the education of local children and that Richard Pooley was a Commonwealth soldier – so the school foundation is 250 years older than this old building.

The main through route is a couple of miles away in the valley of the Lune. Such passing traffic as there is in Wray will, however, come upon the New Inn as the first building at the western entrance to the village. Only the signs will persuade you to hesitate at this plain house. The older part of it is certainly earlier than 1708, and the dining-room has part of the original wattle and daub wall exposed to view. The

21

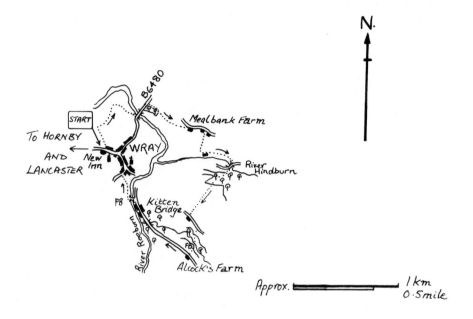

'new' bit that gives it a name was erected in 1775. On the wall of the bar you will find a photograph of a rather severe-looking former landlady who ran the pub before the Second World War – following her own mother in that role – and whose friendly ghost still revisits her former home; the present landlords will be happy to expand on the tale of what happened to the pet monkey. In this part of the world, hare hunting is still carried on and the Vale of Lune Harriers meet at the pub.

Food is available between 12 noon and 2 pm and from 7 pm to 9.30 pm. What is on offer is good, plain fare with steak and kidney pie and top-quality rump steak and T-bone being to the fore. The house pâté is something of a speciality. As this is a freehouse both Boddingtons and Tetley real ales and Symmond's cider are on draught. Drinking hours are 12 noon to 3 pm and 7 pm to 11 pm. Bed and breakfast is available so you can choose not to drive home if you so wish. Families are most welcome, within the pub as well as in the beer garden behind, but, because of the resident dog, owners are asked to check before bringing their own pet into the building.

Telephone: 052 42 21350.

How to get there: The New Inn stands at the western end of the village beside the B6480 off the A683 Lancaster to Kirkby Lonsdale road.

Parking: A large car park is available across the road and there is unlikely to be any problem about leaving your car while you walk if you have a word with the landlord first. If needed, a small amount of additional parking will be found in the village centre near the church.

Length of the walk: 3 miles. Map: OS Landranger 97 Kendal and Morecambe (GR 601676).

The valleys of the Hindburn and Roeburn carve their way south from the Lune into the inaccessible moorlands of the northern flank of the Forest of Bowland. Much of their course is hard to reach and this walk route gives some taste of their attractive nature. In early medieval times the main Lune valley was a border land and settlements like Wray must have represented the first stages of the extension of human activity on to the moorlands.

Just south of the route, beyond Alcock's farm, lies Outhwaite, hidden from prying eyes. Here, it seems, monks ran a mini penal colony where, within living memory, the whipping post, stocks and cell were still to be seen. Well within this century the woodlands provided the raw material for oak-bark swill (basket) makers, bobbin turning and cloggers in Wray, and the mill at Kitten Bridge wove silk for locally made hats.

The Walk

Almost opposite the pub, cross the road and walk in the direction of the Lune along Kiln Lane. This soon becomes a track and in about 100 yards turn right at the crossways; the castle and woods of Hornby are in view. Pass the sewage works fence and continue ahead between hedges of blackthorn and hawthorn and with banks full of flowers – red campion, willow herb, blackberry, vetches – and heavy with the scent of meadowsweet. The path reaches the road by some cottages and you go up to, and over, the new concrete bridge over the river Hindburn. A white-painted up-and-over stile beside the first gate on the right marks the start of the path again, but has no sign on it. Climb the bank behind a small wood of sycamore, pine and ash and follow the old hedge line in the middle of the field to a stile. Away on your left, on a clear day you should see the mass of Ingleborough. Exit on to a lane by the new slurry tank to the left of the buildings of Mealbank Farm – the stile here, unusually, has a dog gate attached. Walk right along the lane 100 yards to Far Meal Bank and turn right between the buildings; there is, once more, no sign. At the field aim left of the first telegraph pole and drop quite steeply to a wicket gate and a sharp bank into the hamlet of Gamblesholme. Bear left along the track behind the buildings and along the access track to a bridge over the Clear beck and then, almost immediately, a bridge which takes you back, on a road, across the river Hindburn.

23

Directly ahead, a sign indicates a path up across the field to a double stile at the wood edge. Bear right up the bank and, as it flattens off, keep half-left to emerge at the far side of the wood, in the corner of a field with the hedge on your left. (There is actually a footpath arrow here, which is only visible from the other direction.) Follow the field edge straight ahead to a lane opposite a barn and turn left; the view behind is particularly wide. Some 300 yards along a lane turns down right into the wood at a sign 'Alcock's Farm'. Take this down to a fine ford over the dipping sandstone rocks of the bed of the Hunt's Gill beck and use the footbridge beside it. Climb up the field to the farm and turn right along the lane. You now drop into the woods along a narrow part of Roeburndale and recross Hunt's Gill beck by a substantial bridge to come to Kitten Bridge Mill and cottages. The little hamlet has been renovated and the show of flowers indicates the care present owners have for it. Just beyond, a large footbridge takes you to the left across the river Roeburn and via a well-made path down river to emerge in Wray beside the school. At the bottom of the brow, turn left along the main street and pass the parish church and the unique memorial to Victoria's Golden Jubilee in 1887 of a lamp held up by the statue of a child. Many of the houses are dated (1694, 1704, and Walnut Cottage is 1673). Go left again at the end, and pass the Methodist church on the left and Duck Street cottages on the right, to return to the New Inn.

Cockerham
The Manor Inn

5

The village name combines the British 'cocker' – meaning winding (and referring to the river) – and the Old English 'ham' – indicating a settlement, so Cockerham has been here a long time and was one of the relatively few Lancashire places mentioned in the Domesday Book (Cochreham). Until recent times the vicar still claimed salmon caught in the ancient traps in the river at certain tides.

Exactly at the junction of roads in Cockerham, the Manor Inn stands where the main road from Lancaster drops down from a promontory in an 8,000 year old shoreline on to the marshlands which lie between the village and the present shore, 1½ miles away. In an endeavour to make it safer,the junction has been widened in recent years and has a shrub-planted island which rather cuts the village in half. The pub began life as a barn in the 16th century and did not take up its present guise until 1878, coming eventually into the hands of Mitchell's, the Lancaster brewers and present owners, in 1926. More recent modernisation has retained its old world look. Eating here covers a wide range, from sandwich and snack to full meals. A hefty farmhouse mixed grill, steak and kidney, or plain steaks will keep the famished on course, or lasagne and a selection of fish dishes should suit those with more delicate appetites. There is a small selection especially for children. Those carrying their own food should ask if they wish to eat in the garden with a drinks purchase. A special of the day is also normally available. Serving times are 12 noon until 2 pm and from 7 pm to 9 pm in the evenings, except for Tuesdays; the pub is open all day on Saturdays. Mitchell's traditional beer is available and the bar stocks Fortress Ale and cider. Families, with or without their well-controlled dogs, are very welcome indeed.

Telephone: 0524 791252.

How to get there: At the junction of the A588 Lancaster to Fleetwood road with the B5272 to Garstang.

Parking: A large car park lies immediately across the road; please have a word at the bar before leaving your car while you walk. As an alternative there is an even bigger public car park 200 yards along the B5272 outside the community hall.

Length of the walk: 5 miles; 5½ miles if you include the circuit to the church. Map: OS Landranger 102 Preston and Blackpool (GR 465522).

This is easy walking with little rise and fall and good ground under foot after dry weather. Inland from the village, and across the shallow valley of the Cocker, the Lancaster Canal contours its way at the very base of the fells of Bowland. The construction of the canal in the 1790s was really an outcome of the long rivalry between Lancaster and Liverpool (which the latter, had they but known this, had already won). The section starting here, at Ellel Grange, was actually the first to be built. The junction with the Glasson Arm (opened in 1826), with its hump-backed bridge designed so that horses did not have to be unhitched when crossing, is a sheer delight.

The Walk

From the front of the pub, walk down the footway along the A588, cross to the other side to the bottom of the hill, and recross to take a path through the field and up to the church; its setting amongst the fields, rather than the houses, makes it most impressive. It may come as a surprise to learn that St Michael's church was mainly rebuilt in 1910 for, as you come towards it from the main road, it stands up above the surroundings as though it has always been there. The church is the effective successor to Cockersand Abbey, which stood by the shore where the river Cocker meets the estuary of the Lune; very little of it is left to see today.

Leave through the main gateway in the direction of the village and cross the end of the large car park to the road. Cross over and turn

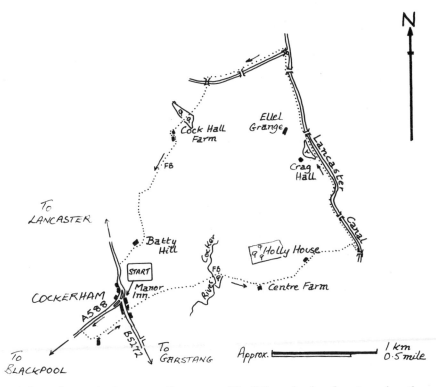

left to the end of a row of cottages (No 27) and take the signed path alongside into the field behind. (This first mile of the walk can be bypassed by walking left out of the pub door along the B5272 to this point.)

At the top of the field the view takes in the Ashton Memorial, in Williamson Park, Lancaster, round the whole west-facing flank of the Bowland fells, with the University of Lancaster below them. Drop down the fields over two stiles to a gate at the right-hand corner of a field and walk round the end of a small wood to a second gate, then ahead under the main power lines to a footbridge over the river Cocker and bear right around the end of a further small wood. The path goes to the right, through the end of the hedge, and then left along it to cross a second field and reach a track just 20 yards left of the buildings of Centre Farm. Go right and then turn left at the corner of the farm buildings and drop gently along a good track with the tower restaurant of Forton motorway services in view ahead. You pass a large wood on the left and then Holly House (with a multitude of sow thistles growing in season out of the yard wall) before swinging right to reach the Lancaster Canal at Potter Brook bridge (No 81). Join the towpath in the Lancaster direction. From time to time you may glimpse the traffic using the A6 on the far side but the canal bank is quiet with ducks a-dabbling and arrowhead and lilies growing from the water. The cottage garden by Hay Carr bridge is very impressive indeed as is the towered elegance of Hay Carr House, set back in the fields. Around Ellel Grange the woods are too dense for you to see much except the top of the church of St Mary and Crag Hall farm; even the small lake is now largely obscured. Unfortunately, Ellel Grange is not on public view though it is said to be one of the finest Italian-style houses in the North-West. The bridge for the hall is different from the others in having a carved stone balustrade, and the next one (No 85) is even more unusual in being double width and divided down the centre because it stands on a boundary. A short and wooded cutting here exposes the underlying sandstone rocks, all green with algal growth.

Suddenly, at the end of the cutting, the scene opens out again and you are at the end of the Glasson Arm of the canal. The lock-keeper's cottage and the surroundings of the lock itself are a picture postcard scene of rural England. Sadly, there is a proposal to cut a new bypass road through the middle of this idyll, though this may remain no more than an idea. Turn left along the Glasson Arm towpath now beside hedges strewn in season with pink bindweed and beneath them wild geraniums and mint. The spire on the low ridge ahead belongs to Thurnham RC church; aim towards it as far as the third bridge (which has iron rails rather than a stone parapet). Cross the bridge to the far side of the canal and take the track which leads below the power pylons and cuts up a short rise through a wood to reach Cock Hall farm. The path does an S through the buildings to a field gate. Bear half-right and drop slightly to a footbridge over a ditch; off to the right you should be able to see Heysham Nuclear Power Station. Continue on the same line to an octagonal water trough in the corner of the field. Walk between hedges for 50 yards and turn left to go along below a distinctive clump of trees on a low ridge on your right. The track leads you to Batty Hill farm and you can then follow the access road to the main A588. Walk along the verge to the left as far as Batty Cottages and then cross to a footway on the far side of the bend. This will lead you round to the traffic island opposite your start at the Manor Inn.

6

Newton by Bowland
The Parkers Arms

Newton by Bowland is an attractive small village with the Parkers Arms as its outstanding building, standing imposingly halfway up the brow, overlooking the bridge spanning the river Hodder. It began life as a gamekeeper's residence attached to Browsholme Hall but its three-part arched windows in the Venetian style suggest it went up in the world some time before taking on its present role. Unusually for this area, the outside is painted black and white but manages to look all of a piece with the sandstone of the surrounding buildings. The gardens are a substantial contributor to the attractiveness of the setting.

The practice of the Parkers Arms is to revise menus on a fortnightly basis so not only will you find specials for the day on offer, but the whole character of the menu alters through the year. When I last called, I found a lengthy list of starters including crudités and lamb kebabs, and a main menu with salmon in two different guises, roast beef and Yorkshire pudding (for which, it appears folk are prepared to travel some distance), and a couple of interesting vegetarian dishes, amongst many others; on occasion roast wild boar can be had. Meals are served from 11 am (12 noon on Sundays) to 3 pm and from 6 pm to 11 pm. The substantial high teas would fit in nicely with the time needed for the suggested walk and, at 4 pm on Sundays, afternoon teas are also served. Overnight accommodation is available so you could choose to begin, or end, your day here. This is a Whitbread house and serves Boddingtons and Flowers real ales and a different guest beer every fortnight. Murphy's stout, Stella Artois lager and wines are on draught. Families are welcome. Because food is served in the bars the policy is not to admit dogs to the building.

Telephone: 020 06 236.

How to get there: The approach is on the B6478 via either Clitheroe or Slaidburn, or via Dunsop Bridge on the Trough of Bowland road.

Parking: Adequate parking is available at the pub by arrangement. A good alternative is to park at the halfway point of the walk as described, at Dunsop Bridge, where there is a public car park (GR 661501); this would then enable you to call at the pub en route.

Length of the walk: 8 miles. Map: OS Landranger 103 Blackburn and Burnley (GR 697503).

This challenging, interesting walk requires a day or, perhaps, an afternoon and long summer evening. There are very few pubs indeed within the Forest of Bowland itself but the Parkers Arms provides a first-class opportunity to walk through the full range of Bowland countryside except for the wildest fells. The upper valley of the Hodder has been much altered by the creation of the Stocks reservoir and Gisburn forest but these middle reaches of the river intermingle the grazing of the valley bottom with small woodlands, the occasional plantation and the moorland edge. Here and there the moorland has still not been driven back too far and the second part of the walk crosses such a stretch. The farms on this route are typically four-square sandstone and, with the notable exception at Foulscales, generally uncompromising.

The Walk

From the pub entrance walk up the brow by the green to the telephone box at the top. Half hidden behind it you will find a sign to 'Pain Hill Moor'. An up-and-over stile leads you between the houses into fields. Go through the gap ahead and along by the wall and walk right of the old hedge line with the moorland of Burn Fell filling the view in front of you. Drop slightly and, at the gate, bear left to stride over the stream and rise to a stile, with crinoid fossils in its steps, so entering a lane. Take two paces only to your left and cross to a further stile hidden behind the opposite hedge (there is no sign here) and make half-right across the field to a gate. Beyond this is a row of sycamores on a walled bank; follow along to the yard of Gamble Hole

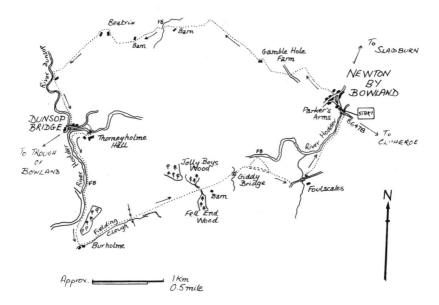

farm and bear left across it to a group of large trees. Once on the far side of them turn half-right on a line parallel to, and about 50 yards from, the stone wall on your right. This will lead you across a large field and between shake holes, where the roofs of small caves have collapsed, to a small gate in the left-hand corner of the top wall at a right-angle bend in Bull Lane.

Follow the track up a little under overhanging thorn hedges to a right-angle left with a view ahead along to the plantations in the Dunsop valley and the lower part of the Trough of Bowland. At the gate, bear half-right and drop down past a barn to cross Rough Syke and a nearby runnel on a flat stone bridge. Follow the right-hand fence round to the corner and aim up just below another barn to join a track which contours round to the two farms at Beatrix. On the far side of the gate beyond the second farm bear right and drop parallel to, and left of, the telephone lines to a stile on to the path beside the river Dunsop. Turn left to the cottages and join the access track to Dunsop Bridge. This village is even smaller than Newton by Bowland but attracts in a different way with its green, the flowers beside the river and the hump-back bridge over the river Dunsop. At the road turn left again and pass the telephone box (marked as the 100,000th in Great Britain and claiming to be in the centre of the country: the points of the compass are marked around it) and car park and toilets.

Go right now, up the drive to Thorneyholme Hall, and cross the iron bridge over the Hodder to a gate on to the bank on the right and

31

walk round the end of the buildings to a track leading down river. The stretch along the Hodder here is particularly rich in wildlife and, with luck, you will see a kingfisher as well as the commoner birds. The path is quite well defined and passes the footbridge which carries the Blackburn Corporation aqueduct of 1882 beneath it. As you pass the end of the wood to the left the route bears away from the river and slightly up to a ford beside Burholme Farm. On the nearside of this take the path up the valley to the left and climb Fielding Clough to an up and over stile on to open grass moorland at a soggy spot beside the wall end. Follow the wall to the corner and strike off across the moor on the same line. Because the moor is convex you will proceed 300 yards or so before two plantations come clearly in sight; aim for the gap in the middle of the wall between them and drop down the fields, past a barn 50 yards to your right, to reach a track at Giddy Bridge. Turn right across Birkett brook and left as far as the cattle grid. This is the access track to Knowlmere Manor and the official footpath drops across the field on the left to the footbridge over the Hodder and then comes back up again about 300 yards further along.

At the lane, turn left and pass Foulscales on the right on the far side of the bridge. At Foulscales the basically 16th century house, with its surprisingly small windows, has the rarity of a garderobe (a privy cantilevered out at first floor level) on its right-hand end. At the barn on the left, 20 yards beyond, go left into the field (there is no sign) and then half-right to drop down across the fields to the bank of the Hodder. The path is clear now beside the river as far as the next bridge. Turn left across it to reach the Parkers Arms in 50 yards.

Calder Vale (Oakenclough)
The Moorcock Inn

7

Calder Vale is as near a functional mill hamlet as you are ever likely to see. Lappet Mill, originally a foundation of the Quaker Jackson brothers in 1835, still operates beside the river with its brass plate, which reads John Lean & Sons, well-worn with polishing, on the door. Girls and men in their work clothes still sit on the wall in the sunshine for a break and a football is still casually kicked around at lunchtime. You can catch a glimpse of the whirling machinery through half-open doors and, for a short while, find the rush and turbulence of the river (from which comes its British name) drowned out by the noise. Many of the workforce live in the rows of stone cottages and the Methodist church presides over the sloping 'square'.

The long range of buildings which make up the Moorcock Inn has stood by the roadside here, at over 225 metres above sea level on the shoulder of the Bleasdale Moors, since the 1670s, at least. Moorcock is another name for the grouse, the shooting of which remains of considerable significance in the area. Once a farm as well as a pub, the inn has original exposed beams and stone walls which give it an atmosphere which is only enhanced by roaring open fires of logs on cold days. Food is served all day at weekends and from 11.30 am to

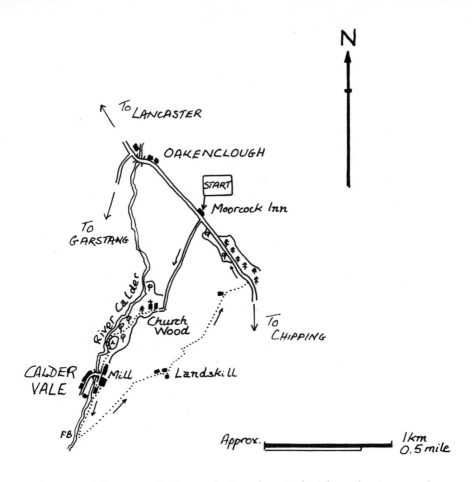

N

To LANCASTER

OAKENCLOUGH

START

Moorcock Inn

To GARSTANG

River Calder

Church Wood

To CHIPPING

CALDER VALE

Mill

Landskill

FB

Approx. |_____| 1 km
                      0.5 mile

3 pm and 7 pm until 11 pm during the week. The selection on the menu is quite extensive and good value, though not attempting anything out of the way. There is no danger of being anything but well satisfied by the soup of the day and, say, gammon and egg with chips, peas and carrots, followed by a good helping of apple pie and cream; roast beef and lamb are something of a Sunday speciality. If this seems too much, the traditional ham and cheese ploughman's lunch will still fill a substantial corner.

As this is a freehouse, Boddingtons and Tetley traditional ales are served every day from 11 am to 11 pm (12 noon to 10.30 pm on Sundays) as well as Moorcock bitter brewed especially for the pub and a couple of ciders on draught. An outside patio does duty for the more commonly found beer garden and gives a glimpse of the views which

characterise parts of the walk; children are welcome here (a reduced menu is available for them) as are well-behaved dogs, and you are likely to find mine hosts amenable to you eating your own food on the patio with a purchase of drinks. There are substantial facilities for parties and, on occasion, you may well find yourself surrounded by dinner or wedding guests. On Wednesday and Friday evenings there is live music in the pub and, on Saturdays, a country and western evening is held in the big lounge.
Telephone: 0995 602130.

How to get there: Calder Vale and Oakenclough are signed from the A6 south of Garstang and Caterall. As an alternative, approach from the crossroads in Galgate village, just south of Lancaster on the A6.

Parking: There is extensive parking at the pub which you will be welcome to use while you walk, but please inform the landlord.

Length of the walk: 3 miles. Map: OS Landranger 102 Preston and Blackpool (GR 542470).

The industrial past of Lancashire, in common with that of the eastern side of the Pennines, began in valleys like these. Today it is more common to find the former mills as ivy-clad ruins amongst woodland or converted into residential accommodation. To be fair, in Lancashire, these will most likely be permanent homes rather than weekend cottages.

The bustle of the village is in considerable contrast to the woodlands around the church of St John the Evangelist (1863) and along the valley sides and the wide open views from above. There are few days in a lifetime when the clarity of the air in any part of Britain enables you to see great distances but I experienced just such a day near Oakenclough when the Calf of Man was quite distinct from the main Isle, 60 miles or more across the Irish Sea.

The final section of the walk also brings the moorland of this western flank of the Forest of Bowland into close focus. This is grouse shooting country, a fact which still limits access to much of the fell land of the Area of Outstanding Natural Beauty. On the route to and from the Moorcock Inn in late summer the blazing colour of the heather must impress and later, as the year begins to die, the fiery red of the bracken sweeps the slopes for miles.

The Walk
Take the lane across the road from the south end of the pub, signed to the church, and walk gently down through fields past Longhouse farm and, as the woods begin, bear right down to the school and church. Take the asphalted path in front of the churchyard and enter the woods beside some large Corsican pine trees to drop down the

35

bank towards the river Calder. Most of the woodland is oak, sycamore, alder and willow and the heavy shade encourages a rich growth of ferns and mosses. Down at the weir village children play and the leet leads off water to the mill pond (with ducks) around which you skirt to reach Calder Vale at Long Row – 19 cottages in total. The square slopes down to the bridge; across the other side is the post office and shop. Continue on the nearside of the river and walk between the mill buildings and the river wall to a farm and go through the buildings to join what can be a rather muddy path along the field beside the river with a small sycamore wood on the left.

At the footbridge turn hard back on your tracks to take a somewhat obscure path beside a ditch up the field, aiming to the left-hand corner of the hedge and fence on the brow above you, where there is a stile. The vegetation changes as you climb up, from the valley pasture to fine-leaved moorland grasses and harebells, with the occasional partridge breaking out of the hedge bottom. Even more unusually, I found here a grey squirrel using the fence as very inadequate cover to cross the open ground. Continue on the same line towards two sets of buildings until you meet a concreted track at the field gate beside a pond on the left. Bear right up the track to the buildings of Landskill with its old stone mullions and drip-courses, dated 1692. At the top of the yard, follow the access track to a right-angled bend and carry on through the gate and along the wall as far as a stone stile on the left 50 yards before the next gate. Climb this and bear half-right towards the buildings of Rough Moor and join the access track at the yard entrance; walk up to the road and turn left along the plantation of larch, spruce and pine to drop back to the Moorcock Inn. At almost any point in this section it is especially worth turning to admire the view – you will have done so from time to time already, I am sure! Depending on your precise position, on a clear day it is possible to see the Langdale Pikes in the Lake District, the Isle of Man and the mountains of North Wales.

St Michael's on Wyre
The Grapes Hotel

8

Two churches on the banks of the river Wyre – St Michael's itself, and St Helen's at Churchtown – are among Lancashire's oldest, and are well worth devoting extra time to take a close look at. The two parishes went to law in the 1200s over the claim that St Michael's took precedence but that claim was lost. Churchtown is, in fact, the mother church of Garstang (which name might well indicate that to the early British this was a sacred place). It may be no accident that the dedication is to St Helen, mother of the Emperor Constantine, who converted the Roman Empire to Christianity, for it was long thought that she was British born. Both places are mentioned in the Domesday Book.

Just to the north of the bridge over the river Wyre, the Grapes Hotel has been serving the passing traveller for some 200 years. The look of the building betrays its origins as a farmhouse and its black and white external decor attracts the eye as you drive through the zigzag bends of St Michael's on Wyre. Food is available between 12 noon and 2.30 pm and 7 pm and 9.30 pm, except on Sunday when the Grapes is open all day from noon until 10.30 pm with a three-course roast special served at lunchtime. Sandwiches, cold salad platters and ploughman's lunches cater for the lighter eater but the more energetic trencherman can choose from a long list of substantial standards, from T-bone steak downwards. A local touch is the fresh Fleetwood haddock – from the docks at the end of the road. The main menu is complemented by a couple of offerings for vegetarians and a children's menu.

Licensed hours are 11 am to 11 pm (10.30 pm on Sunday), with a break 3 pm to 6 pm. This is a Greenalls pub with Thomas Greenalls Original on draught as well as Scrumpy Jack cider. There is a short list of bottled wines and the choice of a house carafe. Families are welcomed and the beer garden is exceptional in having a pet sheep on hand to entertain the youngsters. When the weather permits the use of the garden, you will be welcome also to eat your own food there provided you make a purchase from the bar. Since food is served throughout the premises, dogs are not allowed inside.

Telephone: 099 58 229.

How to get there: On the A586 Garstang to Blackpool road in the village.

Parking: The large car park of the pub is available by request or, if very busy, there is public parking over the bridge and round the corner beside the school.

Length of the walk: 7 miles. Map: OS Landranger 102 Preston and Blackpool (GR 451411).

The walk is right on the edge of the Fylde moss lands and is as nearly flat as could be imagined. As a result, the length of it is less important than it would otherwise seem. Footpaths in these drained mosses are restricted in number since, prior to drainage, there was no practical possibility of there being any, and much of Lancashire's flatlands are comparatively poor walking country. The route includes a couple of stretches of excellent green lane, the second, near Myerscough House Lodge, with, in season, crab apples in abundance in its hedges.

The Walk

Cross the main road and walk north past the garage to the corner by the post office and turn left at the 'Hambleton' sign and go along 50 yards. Cross into Moss Lane (which is metalled), with a footpath sign to 'Nateby' on the corner, and follow it beside hedges of good autumn blackberries and fields of summer 'corn as high as an elephant's eye' to Fairfield farm bungalow. Pass this and take the second gap on the right between the barns (there is no sign) and bear round to the left on a track into a field and then aim slightly left to find an overgrown

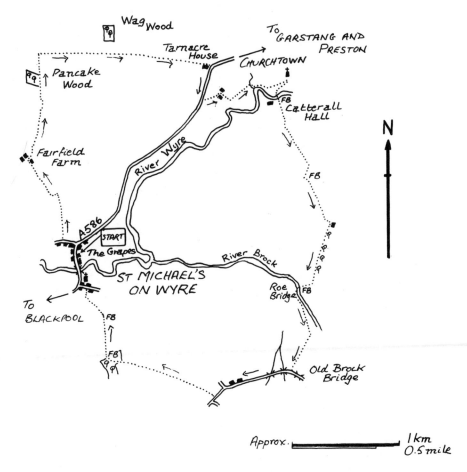

stile in the hedge and continue on the same line across the field to a
gate. The view ahead extends the whole western length of Bowland,
from Ward's Stone behind Lancaster to Beacon Fell and Parlick. Keep
to the left-hand boundary across two further fields, passing the
pheasantry in Pancake Wood on the way, to a green lane.

Turn right along Sharples Lane, with Beacon Fell dead ahead, and
pass the ruin of Moss Side farm to the right and the detached Wag
Wood to the left. Along this stretch, between mixed pasture and arable
fields, I found colonies of the delicious lawyers' wigs fungi. The lane
reaches the A586 at Tarnacre House. Bear right and cross the road to
a footway and take the turn to the left beside a new high wall with a
weathercock just before a white cottage. The formal path runs
through the holiday home called The Orchard but the farmer – busy

39

with a bonfire – assured me that he was happy for me to walk through the yard to a short length of track to a field gate. Once through this, turn left along the hedge to an alloy footbridge and go to the right around the sewage works fence. At the far end St Helen's church comes in to clear view across the field. An iron gate gives access to it at the near end of the hedge. St Helen's building, with its mini spire on the tower, is based on 13th century foundations but appears mainly 15th century, and has inside it unique 17th century wall paintings.

Return to the field and cross the river Wyre on a massively built concrete and steel suspension footbridge and go straight to the access road of Caterall Hall. Where this right-angles to the left, go ahead through an old V-stile and along the left-hand boundary of the field and across the bottom to a footbridge in the right-hand corner (which was in a poor state when I last crossed it). Continue along the right-hand boundary of the next field to the gate at the bottom and go immediately left and right on a metalled lane and past the grey-painted Lodge to a gate into a green lane. Thorn and crab apple trees overshade it from the right and there is a planted shelter belt to the left. Turn right beyond the stile at the end and find a further stile in the field corner on to the flood bank of the river Brock. A few paces left take you to Roe Bridge; cross and turn left along the far bank and drop right on to a track before the second gate. Follow this through to the road beside Old Brock Bridge.

Turn right along the road, taking care for traffic, and walk along over New Brock Bridge and past the Northern Microlight School on the left. At Manor House farm the brick barn is ornately decorated. Just beyond, bear left on the 'Sowerby & Inskip' road and take the gate to the right, opposite the electricity sub-station shortly before the first left turn. Walk along the ditch to the left (filled with hovering dragonflies in summer) to pass a brick bridge on the left and reach a small wood. On the far side is a footbridge. Cross the field end to an iron wicket gate and go right on the nearside of the hedge to a footbridge to the left at the top left-hand corner of the field. The soil is rich, black and (it seems often) ploughed underfoot. Half-left ahead you will see the primary school. Walk towards it and pick up the path between it and the playing field to reach Hall Lane. Turn left and right at the main road to pass St Michael's church before crossing the bridge back to the Grapes. St Michael's is less easy to admire from a distance than St Helen's as it is right beside the main road. Although it is claimed that a church has stood here since AD 640 St Michael's is 13th century in part with the tower as late as 1549. Inside, its breadth and low roof beams make it most attractive and there is some even earlier wall painting and 16th century Flemish window glass.

9 Goosnargh
The Bushells Arms

A Viking from Ireland called something like 'Gosan' (no doubt, with his friend Grim not far away) must have set up his spring and autumn grazing here in the 10th century and left us with the tongue-twisting 'Goozner'. The area is still good grazing land and was, for centuries, a detatched portion of the Fylde parish of Kirkham; thus giving a balance of drier and higher land.

Tucked around the bend of Goosnargh green, the Bushells Arms makes no outward pretence of its hidden strengths, but it is famed far and wide for its food and has been Egon Ronay listed for many years. High popularity means it is wise to book ahead at weekends. A Whitbread house, it carries the usual range of that brewer's beers plus a guest beer. Licensed hours are 11 am to 11 pm. A small beer garden is open in the summer.

Giving an indication of the choice of food available sets aside the matter of quality, which is undoubtedly exceptionally high. The menu has a wide international range. Lunches are served from 12 noon until 2.30 pm and evening meals between 7 pm and 10 pm. Starters include spring rolls, samosas and falafel; the main courses make the mouth water simply to read them. For instance, the old staple, steak and kidney pie, is here cooked with stout and served with potatoes with peppers, garlic, cream, Parmesan cheese and spices. Chicken Olympus has a filling of bacon, asparagus and grated cheese bound in a hollandaise sauce and all wrapped in puff pastry. Vegetarian dishes include home-made baked beans. Puddings and specials of the day do, of course, vary. If you really prefer something light, then salads and ploughman's lunches are served. Children are welcome and there is a small special menu for them.

Telephone: 0772 865235.

How to get there: Follow the sign for 'Goosnargh Village' from the B5269 Broughton (A6 to Preston) to Longridge road and find the Bushells Arms on the inside of the bend at the top end of Goosnargh green, almost opposite the lane to the school and church.

Parking: There is limited parking outside the pub itself but plenty of public parking is available beside the green and in the school lane.

Length of the walk: 3½ miles. Map: OS Landranger 102 Preston and Blackpool (GR 559368).

A glance at the 1:25 000 Pathfinder map (No 679 Preston North) shows that the area around Goosnargh is full of small ponds — a considerable contrast with much of the rest of the country, where they have been filled in since the last war — and the walk route passes at least five of them. It is also clear that the fields here (in the past at least) have been relatively small compared with the much bigger ones out on the Fylde plain.

The Walk
Turn left from the pub doorway and follow the road along the top of the green (now a sports field) until it bends to the right. Immediately ahead, a sign points through the garden of a bungalow called Rockley and to a path which skirts the garden fences to enter a field beside a pond filled with yellow flag. Follow the left-hand hedge to a stile on to a track almost opposite a decaying Second World War brick-built hut. (In the height of summer, this path can be overgrown and you may prefer to stay with the road as far as the first farm on the right and to turn left down the track to reach the same point.) Continue on the line of the track and then over a series of stiles past another pond — where it may be muddy after rain — to the B5269. Turn right and, almost immediately, go left down the access track of Chingle Hall. Pass a third pond on your left and then Chingle House on the right with a bow fan-light over the door. The way wanders left, then right past a converted brick barn and Chingle Hall itself will be obvious on the

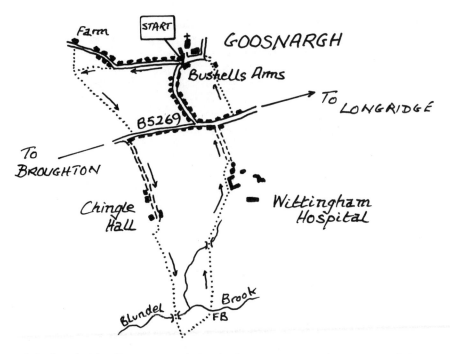

right-hand side. Entrance to it is via the caravan on the corner of the car park.

Chingle Hall lays claim, with some justice, to being the oldest occupied brick-built house in England (the outside is rendered so it is not immediately apparent that it is brick). Erected in 1260, probably on the site of an earlier farmhouse, it is one of only 20 moated houses in the country where the moat survives – as do its fishponds. From the establishment of the Church of England in 1670 until Catholic emancipation in 1829, Chingle Hall was a haven for priests and has at least three hides for them and another three for documents. Its chapel was rediscovered in 1962 and is now dedicated for both RC and C of E worship. There is also a claim that it is England's most haunted house, including the ghost of St John Wall! Born at the Hall in 1620 he was, like many another Catholic son, sent to Douai, in France, to be educated as a missionary priest and worked in the Midlands before being martyred at Worcester in 1679. Friends are said to have taken his head to France but then to have returned it to Chingle Hall at the time of the Revolution, in 1789. Cromwell reputedly used the roof as a lookout before the battle of Preston. It is open Monday to Saturday in the afternoon from Easter to October and from 10 am on Sundays (telephone 0772 861082).

On leaving Chingle Hall, continue on the access track round to the right and use the left-hand iron gate to pass a further pond beside the track. Once in the field proper, keep to the left-hand boundary – passing a fifth pond to your right – and look for the stile in the bottom left-hand corner. Once over this, keep ahead past the oak tree at the top of the bank and drop down to the bridge over the Blundel brook. The track rises slightly and then flattens off and, in 50 yards, turn at right-angles to the left and cross the field to a much overgrown stone stile in the hedge. Aim towards the water tower in the distance and drop down the field, back towards the brook, and recross it on a substantial footbridge. Rise up a little (with the buildings of Wittingham Hospital in sight) along a line of oaks and continue across the field to drop slightly into the top of a wooded clough and walk through to a wicket gate into the far field. Angle diagonally right for the corner of the brick-built farm buildings and turn along the outside of them. Proceed along the field boundary, past the shelter belt of trees which screens the main buildings of the hall, until you are about 20 yards short of the corner of the field. The path continues on the right-hand side of the fence, over a short length of non-barbed wire – difficult to spot – to join the hospital access road. Walk along this to the lodge beside the main road. Wittingham Hospital was once the second largest psychiatric hospital in Europe, with its own railway link and as many as seven estate farms to supply it, but is now due for closure.

Cross the road to the footway and turn right as far as a footpath to the left between the houses. In the field to the rear, walk across, on a line well right of the church tower, to the near corner of a house garden and cross right through the fence on to the entrance driveway. Continue down to the lane and bear left past Bushell Hospital to return to the Bushells Arms.

The local parson, Dr Bushell, willed the building of the Bushell Hospital in 1722, and it still serves the elderly: the obelisk dates from 1844. The major proportion of the large church of St Mary is 16th century, though small portions may be older. The projection from the massive tower contains a stairway. The pub on the corner, the Grapes, makes some claim to continuity with an alehouse in Goosnargh at the time of Domesday. Celebration of one sort or another has certainly been a fashion in the village and the locals are said to have baked 10,000 'Goosnargh cakes' (recipe not recorded) for Prestonians on Good Friday Sunday school picnics late last century.

10 Heapey
The Red Cat

Heapey as a name goes back to at least the early 1200s and seems to indicate an enclosure surrounded by hedges rich in roses and, therefore, rose fruits (hips). Wheelton, the adjoining large village, is a Victorian upstart built around a mill (the mill is gone – destroyed in a fire) but has equally old origins.

How long the Red Cat has stood beside the main road from Chorley to Blackburn is impossible to say; the building bears no date but looks basically mid-19th century with several higgledy-piggledy additions. The origin of the pub name is equally obscure. The stone-flagged small bar has a cosy atmosphere and the adjacent conservatory, through which you enter, is most unusual in a pub building. (I remember, years ago, being very grateful for it when the rain was sluicing, two inches deep, down the road outside.) Though its address is Heapey, it is so close to the parish boundary that it is, in effect, the first building in Wheelton village. The present owner is Scottish & Newcastle Breweries (this is a Matthew Brown pub); licensed hours are 11.30 am to 11.30 pm with an extension for restaurant meals. Theakston Best Bitter is on draught, together with Guinness, McEwans lager and Beck's beer as well as chilled wine. Food here is in the Italian style,

45

and the restaurant wine list carries no less than 14 Italian wines, as well as others. Something very different as a starter is fresh grilled sardines, though I might be very tempted by home-made minestrone soup given the slightest excuse (nothing like the tinned stuff). Pasta, pizza and pollo (chicken) form the bulk of the interesting menu, complemented with a variety of steaks. The simplicity of pollo arrosto (chicken breast roasted with rosemary) is very attractive but it is hard to bypass Red Cat special steak (fillet with smoked bacon and blue cheese) – or almost everything else on offer. If you really do feel you must eat lightly the bar snacks, be it sandwiches, steak and kidney pie, or filled baked potatoes, will satisfy. There is a family dining area and a garden play area for children next to the beer garden. As food is served everywhere it is impractical to allow dogs inside.

Telephone: 0257 263966.

How to get there: The pub lies beside the A674 about 1 mile on the Blackburn side of junction 8 on the M61 to the north of Chorley, just beyond the end of the dual carriageway section. Access is via the lane signed to the left to 'Wheelton' and first left along the (old) Blackburn Road – so it has, in a sense, moved from one side of the road to the other over the years.

Parking: There is a very large car park which you will be welcome to use so long as you inform the pub staff.

Length of the walk: 4 miles. Map: OS Landranger 102 Preston and Blackpool (GR 597207).

The route is mildly up and down for the first half with a long second section being flat along the canal, and a final short rise. This stretch of the Leeds and Liverpool Canal is particularly interesting for the series of seven locks which enables boats to rise up Johnson's Hillock and the junction, by the bottom lock, with the Lancaster Canal (actually beyond Town Lane where the route turns back uphill). The latter ran only as far as Walton Summit and was never linked direct across the Ribble to the main canal north of Preston, so cargoes had to be transferred by tramway.

The Walk

Drop down the line of the old Blackburn Road past the beer garden and cross the A674 direct into Tanhouse Lane. Pass Fig Tree House on the right along a metalled section and walk up the brow into the farmyard ahead, towards a brick barn. Turn left in the yard to a field gate. Go through this and up the right-hand boundary and, at the corner of the hedge, bear up a little between the house and the bungalow to exit on to a footway via a stile at the corner of the garden

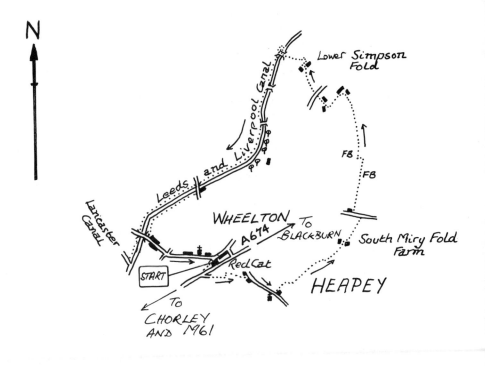

N

Lower Simpson Fold

Leeds and Liverpool Canal

Lancaster Canal

FB

FB

WHEELTON
A674
To BLACKBURN

South Miry Fold Farm

Red Cat

START

HEAPEY

To CHORLEY AND M61

Approx. 1 km
0·5 mile

of the latter. Walk right up the hill and pass St Barnabas church, Heapey (now a joint parish with Brinscall). The church's origins seem to have been in the late 1600s, but it has been much altered over the years. Cross over the lane to a path beside Laburnum Cottage and drop steeply down the left-hand fence to a stile in a boggy patch at the bottom of a valley far too large to have been formed by the present minute stream (it has to be an Ice Age relic); way to the right are the moors of Anglezarke above White Coppice. Climb up now, left of the broken hedge of hollies, to a stile to the right by the lone oak tree. At the next gate go left and aim to the buildings of South Miry Fold farm ahead. Join the track and move across to the right-hand access road and walk up it to a lane.

Cross over and go left 20 yards to a footway. In 5 yards you will find a wicket gate to the right just before a house (this bears an apparently meaningless sign – 'beware of the bull') Follow the left-hand boundary the length of two fields to a footbridge; cross over the middle of the next field on the same line to a stile and then go left to a second footbridge. Walk up the left-hand boundary to the top of the brow until the chimney of Withnell Fold comes into sight half-right (the Conservation Area there is worth a visit) and proceed between the fences and over the stile at the bottom right-hand corner of the field. The path now crosses a short access way to the field to the right (with a new building on the far side of it) by two stiles in quick succession and drops down wooden steps to enter the garden of a converted barn beside the garage. Turn left and go through the orchard to cross a field track behind a farm by another pair of stiles and go along the fence on the right as far as the hen runs. At the far end of these, hollies in a house garden overhang an old track and half hide the stile to the right. Over this the way is built up beside an open drain and requires a little care until you reach the access track which leads down past Higher Simpson Fold to the main road.

Cross with care to a stile and bear slightly right across the field to a footbridge and a stile beside a barn at the entrance of the yard of Lower Simpson Fold. Walk ahead through the yard and skirt round the slurry pit in the field beyond to the right. Use the stile beside the gate and immediately go back left over a second stile into a small triangle of land which funnels down to a bridge over the canal. Turn right over the bridge and immediately right again over a stile and on to the towpath; follow this back under the bridge and along beneath stone bridges Nos 84 and 83 and pass the woods and duck farm at Prospect House on the far side. In the garden of Prospect House the rotunda above six columns is the top of the tower of the former Wheelton church which has been rebuilt.

You will come now to Wheelton Boat Club moorings and a yard on the far side where you can buy a converted narrow boat if you wish, and then reach the Top Lock pub. From this point it is possible to continue on either side of the canal – though the towpath is the easier – as far as the next bridge. The towing horses had to come up to the road here because the towpath does not continue under the bridge itself. (If you wish to view the junction with the Lancaster Canal, carry on a few hundred yards and then return.) Come up to the road yourself and turn up the hill along the footway of Town Lane and pass Hall Square on the right and then St Chad's RC church and school on the left. St Chad's is a recent oddity with a Romanesque small tower. Its origins, like those of St Barnabas, date back to the 1600s.

From the church return to Blackburn Road and the Red Cat.

⑪ Hesketh Bank
The Becconsall Hotel

Hesketh Bank and adjacent Tarleton have slowly grown since the Second World War as commuters and retirees have filled in between what was recorded as 'rough and ready, primitive... one long and bewildering street, and all sizes of houses' late last century, and have submerged the earlier hamlet of Becconsall. The buildings are all strung out along the top of a rise which represents a former sea (or perhaps lake) shoreline looking out over saltmarsh lands which were reclaimed from the Ribble estuary between 1810 and 1883. The main driving purpose of the work was to make the Ribble navigable for bigger vessels up to the port of Preston (which finally closed in 1983) but it also created rich agricultural lands behind the sea banks. As late as the 1870s guides took people across the estuary ford to Warton. Hesketh Bank gets its modern name from the family of the major promoter of the works but Becconsall takes us back a thousand years to one of the many Norsemen who came, via Ireland, to this dry hillock amongst the marshes.

The present, rather massively built, two-storey, red-brick building of the Becconsall Hotel, with a vaguely Tudor inspiration, replaces an earlier three-storey one which burnt down some time after the First

World War (there was, clearly, then the hope that Hesketh Bank's aspirations of becoming a resort would materialise). The spacious interior presents a more welcoming aspect and I can well believe the overnight accommodation on offer is as comfortable as any. Opening times for food are 12 noon to 2.30 pm and 6 pm to 9.30 pm Tuesday to Saturday, noon to 9.30 pm on Sundays and at lunchtime only on Mondays. I always look for something with a local touch on a pub menu and the gammon grilled with Lancashire cheese is a speciality here which I have not come across elsewhere. Their own recipe mushroom Stroganov makes a different starter too. An extensive choice characterises the menu as a whole and should satisfy the children, vegetarians, and light eaters of the party without difficulty; specials of the day add further variety.

The Becconsall is a Tetley house so serves Tetley bitter and Skol lager; both Strongbow and Merrydown cider are available on draught. Licensing hours commence at 11 am and a restaurant licence extends drinking time until midnight. Families are particularly welcome and there is plenty of space in the beer garden for children. If it is an occasion on which you prefer to carry your own food please do check about eating it on the premises when buying your drinks.

Telephone: 0772 815314.

How to get there: Turn right off the A59 just west of the crossing of the river Douglas, signed for 'Tarleton' and 'Hesketh Bank', or approach from the Plough roundabout at the northern boundary of Southport via Banks. The hotel is on Station Road immediately north of the old railway bridge.

Parking: The hotel car park is extensive and you are unlikely to find it crowded, but should this be the case, there is side road parking within a few yards.

Length of the walk: 3½ miles; a series of parallel paths make it possible to reduce the length to 3 miles or increase it to 5½ miles. Map: OS Landranger 102 Preston and Blackpool (GR 447228).

The Ribble estuary is a haunt of waterfowl at all times of the year and most of it is either National Nature Reserve or Wildfowl Reserve. The remaining saltmarshes on its bank are grazed and attract a different spectrum of birds. The best time of year for migrants – ducks, geese and waders – is September and October, the worst June and July. It is worth checking the Liverpool tide tables (available from James Laver Printing Co., Argyle Street, Liverpool 1) to try to reach the outer banks about half an hour before high tide.

Until the late 1960s a railway ran from Southport to Preston and crossed the

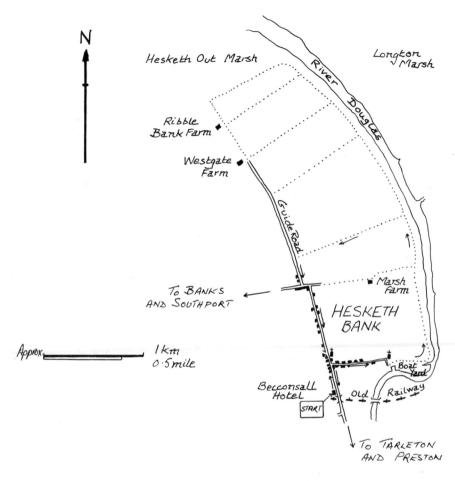

Douglas at Becconsall. All that is left are the road bridge, the bridge over the river and the station yard, now the headquarters for a firm of builders' merchants. In the back of the yard, however, half hidden round the corner, is the base of the West Lancashire Light Railway. Narrow gauge (2 ft) locomotives and stock from quarries and docks locally, and around the world, are operational at weekends (Hon. Sec. telephone 0942 218078).

The Walk

Whether you adopt the route I suggest, and return via the second of the parallel paths across the reclaimed fields, or extend your walk right out to the edge of Hesketh Out Marsh will, I suspect, relate to how much time you spend bird-watching, and that will depend on both

51

weather and season. A decision will also be needed as to whether or not to visit the West Lancashire Light Railway first or last. It is located about 100 yards across the road in the opposite direction to the walk route.

Leave the hotel car park along the footway to the left and cross the road into Becconsall Lane. On the way you will pass Lancashire's Hedgehog Rescue – a supportive call will be of interest to some. The lane runs past pleasant suburban housing until it drops down towards the river, past Becconsall Hall farm on the left. All Saints old church is immediately ahead. The old church (1764), with its little bellcote, is now forlornly abandoned in its graveyard. Its successor (1926) stands impressively on Station Road. It is possible to detour through the graveyard to reach the riverside path at the boat yard, then turn left and climb on to the near bank of the drained levels. The route now follows the bank top beside the river Douglas (or Asland).

Along the river a couple of boat yards and moorings still serve sea-going craft and there is a marina at the lock on the end of the canal at the Preston end of Tarleton. On the far side of the river are the salt-marshes of Longton Marsh with the obvious, isolated building by the bank of the Dolphin pub. The view is wide all round, from Winter Hill, to the south-east, round through Darwen Tower to the hills of Bowland. Anywhere along this bank you can expect to view a variety of birds. To extend the possibility to the maximum requires walking round the corner and beside Hesketh Out Marsh to return past Ribble Bank and Westgate farms.

The suggested route passes a pasture and then the sewage works, with its screen of poplars, and continues as far as the remains of a cross fence on the bank. On the far bank is the mound of a Lancashire County Council rubbish dump with its attendant clamour of gulls. Down to the left is a stile beside a stone-arched culvert within which there is a flood-control gate. Walk between the fields of cabbages, carrots, sprouts, beetroot and cauliflower (all, or any of them) past small packing sheds, gangs of pickers, and men driving dumpers full of chicken manure, to reach Guide Road at a bridge beside some greenhouses. Turn left to join Shore Road opposite old brick cottages.

Go left and bear to the right at the corner up to The Brow and use the footway along Station Road past exhortions to buy bedding plants from small nurseries. Beside the village hall are pitches for cricket and rugby and the bowls club and, immediately after, is the new All Saints church. The hotel is now in sight a few hundred yards ahead on the right.

12 Scarisbrick
Heaton's Bridge Inn

Scarisbrick is one of those parishes where there is really no one centre but rather a scattering of small villages and hamlets of which the group of dwellings, workshops and farms around Heaton's Bridge is one. The bridge was so named when the cutting of the canal divided land belonging to a farmer called Heaton and the pub has stood beside it since it was built in 1847, beside an old manure wharf on the canal with a brick tower Second World War 'goon box' on guard over it. No doubt the buildings of earlier times were mostly quite insubstantial but there is a brick house, with stone quoins, just along from the pub marked 'HH RH 1749'.

The pub building itself, of dark brick, gives an impression of tidy neatness and the present landlord has made considerable efforts to enhance its general attractiveness. The modernised inside has maintained this cosy air and the steady trade at lunchtimes emphasises his success; food is not served in the evening. The policy is to provide all lunches at a very attractive single price; meals are available between 12 noon and 2 pm. The menu is made up of what might be regarded as the good old standards – gammon, cod, roast chicken, scampi and steak pie – together with a grill which includes Lancashire black

pudding. The daily specials add some more variety. The bar is open from 11.30 am to 11 pm Monday to Saturday and from 12 noon to 3 pm and between 7 pm and 10.30 pm on Sundays. A feature is made of double spirit measures at a single measure price in the early evening. A Tetley house, Walker Best Bitter and Tetley Mild are on draught, as is Gaymer's Old English cider; wine is available. Part of the forecourt has been made into a tabled patio and families with children are most welcome there. The policy is to allow well-behaved dogs in the bar, but it is wise to forewarn the staff first.
Telephone: 0704 840549.

How to get there: The pub is on the southern side of the canal bridge on the B5242 Burscough to Southport road.

Parking: There is a large car park which you will be welcome to use when going for your walk.

Length of the walk: 3 miles. Map: OS Landranger 108 Liverpool (GR 404118).

This is very easy walking with only a gentle rise up on to Mill Brow by the Pumping Station. Much of it is on lanes or towpath and the soil drains quickly, so mud should not usually prove a problem.

This area of low hillocks (from which the parish derives its name) has been settled, amongst the waters and marshes which formed the now-drained Martin Mere, for more than a thousand years; on autumn days you will probably hear (and see) the skeins of geese flying to and from the Wildfowl and Wetlands Trust reserve on the remains of the mere just a mile or two away. Our earliest record is of Roman coins found in the field to the left-hand on the northern side of Heaton's Bridge.

The latter part of the walk is through the Conservation Area of Pinfold – there is an information map on the way down to the towpath from the Red Lion bridge – and ends beside the woods and fields of the park of Scarisbrick Hall.

The Walk
Turn right in front of the pub and walk along to the sign for 'Village Hall' at the corner of Smithy Lane where notices for everything from pansies to tomatoes emphasise the richness of the fine silt soils here. Turn right along the footway and continue as far as the Mission church (the church of the Good Shepherd, Hurlston Green). Go left, now, along Moorfield Lane and cross to the footway in front of some modern detached houses and pass cottages dated variously between 1828 and 1898 to a footpath and stile to the right at the bend in the road. Walk behind the stables and turn left on the far side of the young shelter belt of trees beyond them. Continue round the outside of the

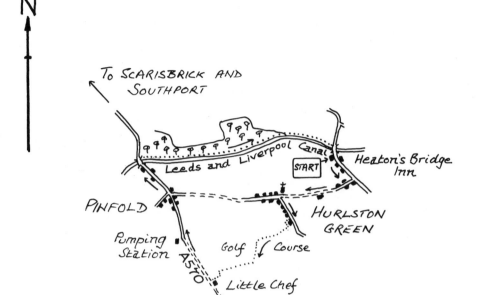

N

To SCARISBRICK AND SOUTHPORT

Leeds and Liverpool Canal

START

Heaton's Bridge Inn

PINFOLD

Pumping Station

A570

HURLSTON GREEN

Golf Course

Little Chef

To ORMSKIRK

Approx. [========] 1 km
0·5 mile

paddock fence and go between the hedge and ditch to reach a track on the edge of a new golf course – yet another change in land use.

Drop a little to the bridge over the Hurlston brook and climb up a few feet to a bend in the track. Immediately left you will see a large pond. Turn off left to walk beside this and go forward about 20 yards more to a clump of beech trees. The path turns at right-angles to the right here and goes across two fairways (beware of speeding golf balls) to a newly planted belt of trees on the far side. Amongst these is a parallel zigzag of hawthorn hedges which leads through to a gate in a wire fence. Turn left along the outside of the fence to the trees behind the Little Chef, which occupies the site of the former Mill Brow farm.

The path runs down the side of the field nearest the car park to exit on to the A570 beside the entrance. Cross over and walk right along the footway. You will shortly pass Mill Brow Pumping Station, one of the few left which are still working to keep the mosses drained. A windmill which stood beside it in the past gave its name to this low hillock. The view is almost 360° around – behind you is the tower of Aughton church and in front is that of Scarisbrick Hall. Today this is a school and the only opportunity to visit is on open days in the summer. The family was here as early as the 13th century but the present building, with its huge clock tower, is a 19th century creation of the architects Pugin, father and son (who worked also on the Houses of Parliament).

You drop back down into Pinfold past a cottage of 1804, and Quarry House with its herd of goats and milk, yoghurt and cheese for sale. The hamlet of Pinfold contains some amazing buildings – the smithy with its Roman portico and statues in niches, and the former wheelwright's shop (now a house) with its massive finial on the gable – which must have been associated with the early work on the Scarisbrick estate. Just a few yards down Pinfold Lane is a 14th century thatched cottage which gives an indication of the better quality housing of earlier centuries. The pinfold itself is where wandering cattle were impounded until claimed.

Cross the bridge and drop left on to the towpath and come back under to go along the Scarisbrick woods to return to Heaton's Bridge past moorings with boats like *Casuarina* – why an Australian shrub? – and the more obvious *Quiet Waters* and a large caravan site on the far side.

13 Dalton, near Upholland
Ashurst Beacon Inn

The maps are consistent in spelling the name of the Beacon itself with an apostrophe but the pub does well enough without and stands at the roadside at the top of the climb up from Newburgh where the road flattens off to run southwards along the ridge to Upholland. It is a welcoming and popular place and well known around for its ales and bar and restaurant food. It is the starting point for many a short walk on to the public access land of the adjacent beacon. There appears to be no indication on the building of its age but it is certain that a pub hereabouts is no newcomer. Food is available all day, seven days a week (12 noon to 10.30 pm on Sundays). The menu has been constructed with the idea in mind of offering tastes from around the world with gammon, roast chicken, mixed grill and trout representing the tradition of Britain and chilli con carne and curries, amongst others, taking you farther afield. A ploughman's lunch or salads cater for those who want to fill a corner rather than the whole person and there are dishes suited to vegetarians.

Only real ales are served here – Theakston, Wells, Robinson's and Moorhouses Pendle Witches. Guinness, Gillespie's Malt Stout and Strongbow cider are on draught. The Beacon is unusual in having an

57

area inside set apart for family use, though there is also a beer garden available when weather permits. Customers with dogs are asked not to bring them into the bar but are welcome to have them with them in the outside areas if on a lead.

Telephone: 0695 632607.

How to get there: The approach is either from Upholland, turning for Newburgh from the A577 at the top of the hill, or from Newburgh from the B5239 (the Burscough to the M6 – junction 27 – road) along the lane signed 'Dalton' at the eastern end of the village before reaching the traffic lights on the bridge.

Parking: At the pub when there is room, or in the public car park overlooking the golf course 100 yards in the Newburgh direction (there is no sign at the car park entrance and it is easy to miss).

Length of the walk: 2½ miles. Map: OS Landranger 108 Liverpool (GR 501076).

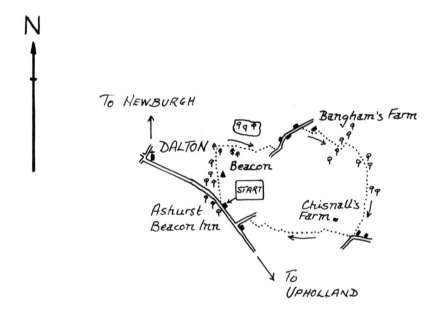

58

The edge of the Greater Manchester conurbation is quite sharply delimited but, despite being so close to it, the walk route takes you through some very pleasant, slightly hilly country with urban Wigan often in sight.

The eastern slopes of the ridge remain farmland, even though they are well within sight of the urban expanse of Wigan and sound of the steady roar of traffic on the M6. Many of the farm buildings, barns and outhouses are of sandstone and betray some age (though few are dated). At the bottom of the western slope lies the new town of Skelmersdale – much of it visible from the public car park. Associated with this, West Lancashire District Council has developed a Country Park which is – perhaps rather confusingly – known as Beacon Park although it lies just to the right of the road about a mile in the Upholland direction from Ashurst's Beacon. At Beacon Park there is an information centre with small displays about the natural history of the area and from which guided walks are run from time to time.

The Walk

A short access track at the northern end of the pub building leads on to the open grassland, surrounded by scrub woodland, which encircles the obelisk on Ashurst's Beacon; walk across to the western face of the obelisk. Ashurst's Beacon is the highest point (around 160 metres) of a ridge of sandstones and shales which runs from Billinge (near St Helens) north to fade out into the lowlands around Mawdesley. The river Douglas cuts through the ridge in the gap between the Beacon and Parbold Hill. The monument was built in 1798 when, as in the days of the Spanish Armada, it was thought necessary to provide a means of rousing the country in defence by using a chain of beacon fires. Quite how this could be done using such a structure is, to say the least, somewhat obscure! The site takes its name from the hall (1649), which belonged to the Ashurst family, and stands just behind the late Victorian Dalton church. The view from the Beacon on a clear day is, undoubtedly, one of the finest in the county and largely explains the stone plaque which records the gift of the site to the people of Wigan in 1962; it is said you can see 16 counties from here. As long ago as 1670, Roger Lowe was writing '. . . the pleasantest place I ever saw, a most gallant prospect . . .'.

After pausing to take in the view westwards – from North Wales to The Lakes on a clear day – continue more or less straight on to pass a bench and enter the scrub woodland. At the stile in the corner bear right amongst pines, beech and oak and follow round to the right into a field. The view ahead is now up the valley of the river Douglas with Appley Bridge village across on the far slope and the Gathurst motorway viaduct in the distance. The Douglas river gap has served as a major route for trade for centuries. The river itself was made navigable for small craft and was then supplanted by the Leeds and Liverpool Canal. This, in turn, gave way to the railway; oddly enough the main road routes stick to the high ground and, even today, no convenient road uses the gap itself.

The path is clear across the grass and passes close to a small wood on the right and a more substantial wood downslope to the left, and then drops to a stile and footbridge in a small clough. Follow the left-hand boundary of the field on the far side to reach a metalled lane at the bottom right-hand corner. You can actually see the underlying thin-bedded sandstones exposed in the path down the bank.

Turn to the left down the lane between high banks of ivy, fern and foxglove and walk through the refurbished buildings of Caterall's farm to a track to the right opposite a white house, almost hidden by trees. The path leads around the right-hand boundary of Bangham's farm and to a grassy track beside a row of Lombardy poplars beyond it. Signs in the next field lead you between old fences into a wooded clough in which you will need to stride over the stream. At the top of the far bank go left about 20 yards, to the corner of the field and turn to the right along the lower side of an old boundary ditch. The ditch soon fades out but continue to the corner of the field and through the copse to emerge on to a substantial track.

Turn to the left and follow this across the open field until it bends left at right-angles beside a small wood. At this point, continue dead ahead up the slope of a narrow field towards two houses at the top. Keep to the right-hand side and go through a gap in the Leyland cypress hedge and use the driveway which runs to the right behind the house (this seems a little disconcerting at first but your right-of-way will be confirmed by the sign at the bend of the lane at the entrance gateway). Immediately to the right is a farm access track. Use this to walk past the dairy at Chisnall's farm, 100 yards away to the right, and follow the track round to the left to a single ash tree in the centre of a triangle of grass where tracks meet. Bear round to the left to the first field entrance on the right and turn up the slope on the near side of the hedge which runs at right-angles from the track up the slope; the remains of an old stone stile just off the track will confirm the route start beside a very small (and well-silted) pond. Climb up over the top of the field and go left through the gap in the corner and then along the other side of the same hedge line to a path between hedges from the field corner. On the left is Dalton cricket field and you will soon reach a metalled lane beside a go-kart track behind the Prince William pub. Turn left and walk 150 yards to a T-junction and go right for the short distance to the Ashurst Beacon Inn.

Haskayne
The Ship Inn

14

Except that it is a British name, I have been unable to find out anything certain about the derivation of 'Haskayne' – could it be related to hazels growing on this very low sandstone knoll amongst the marshes? The Ship Inn is a great favourite with those who enjoy sitting beside canals and watching the world go by. The section of the Leeds and Liverpool Canal which passes by here was the first to be completed and the Ship likes to think of itself as the oldest pub on the canal. Food is available both lunchtimes and evenings. Lunch is served from noon until 2 pm each day and evening food from 6 pm to 8.45 pm except for Sundays, when service begins at 7 pm. In summer the place is open all day on Saturdays. The menu is a straightforward one but you are warned that the lamb curry is hot. The list quietly hides a better than usual choice for vegetarians and the choice of half a dozen salads daily is more than most. Children have their own menu. Families are welcome here and there is both a family room and a beer garden. The Ship is a Tetley house and serves Tetley traditional ales.

Telephone: 0704 840572.

How to get there: The Ship is on Rosemary Lane, less than ½ mile from the Haskayne crossroads with the A567 (Liverpool to Southport road).

61

Parking: Walkers are welcome to use the fair-sized pub car park. Should it prove to be full, there is further parking in the direction of the village beside the canal.

Length of the walk: The suggested route is 8 miles; a shorter loop is 6½ miles (marked S on the sketch map) and a longer 10 miles (marked L on the sketch map); the Haskayne Cutting Reserve loop is a 1½ mile saunter which can be added if you wish – or can be your walk if you want to take things very easy. Map: OS Landranger 108 Liverpool (GR 364081).

Using the Ship as a base gives opportunity for a variety of route choices through similar countryside. Although the suggested walk distance is relatively long the routes are a gentle wander. Apart from bridges, the land is virtually flat and, with the possible exception of the two fields near the Scotch Piper, the surface underfoot is always firm and dry which makes for easier than usual progress. Until relatively recently there was no practical circuit across these moss lands unless almost entirely on roads. Even now this remains partly so but the creation of the Aintree to Ainsdale Cheshire Lines Path along the old railway line by the SUSTRANS organisation (it works to develop non-vehicle routes nationwide and can be contacted at 35 King Street, Bristol BS1 4DZ) has made it possible at last.

The Leeds and Liverpool Canal is one of the oldest (it was started in 1770) and is certainly the longest (at 127 miles) in Britain and is the only one crossing the Pennines still navigable. It was a very profitable enterprise and cargo traffic did not cease until 1972. Along the canal you are sure to find many anglers quietly wrestling with their potential quarry. The banks are rich with flowers and fruits in season. Duck, moorhen and coot will certainly be on the water with swans and the occasional heron. A whole variety of bridge types cross it. At Downholland Cross you will pass the Scarsbrick Arms up on the bridge and, a little beyond, the obviously old farm of Downholland Hall. The tower of St Thomas' church (1841), Lydiate, is quite clear on the left throughout much of the walk.

The Walk
Leave the car park to the left and walk along the footway of Rosemary Lane towards the village of Haskayne. Cross over the A567 at the crossroads by the Kings Arms to the corner of School Lane where there is a small blue 'Cheshire Lines' sign. Divert round the Haskayne Cutting loop by turning right along the footway of the main road as far as the first turn to the left at the Blue Bell pub. At the railway bridge take the path to the left along the edge of the reserve and cross back over the fields to the village. The Haskayne Cutting Nature Reserve is owned by Lancashire Wildlife Trust. Access permits for the cutting itself are available from the Trust at Cuerden Park Wildlife Centre, Shady Lane, Bamber Bridge, Preston PR5 6AU, but the public footpath

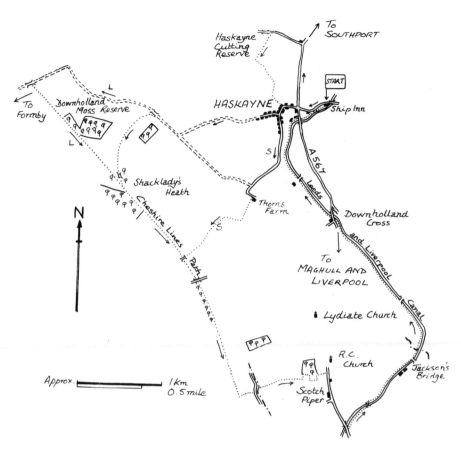

runs beside it and enables you to see some of the plant and bird life.

If not taking the diversion continue ahead past the Old Post Office and craft centre to the thatched-roofed Stock Cottage on the bend, with its outside stone steps. Bear round to the left past the shops and walk to the corner of Riding Lane. Turn right and walk out of the village by some suburban homes to an unfenced lane between arable fields of cabbage, carrots, potatoes, barley and beans. At the T-junction turn right on the lane, from which vehicular traffic is currently barred, and follow the track to the left beside the old railway bridge to join the former railway track and walk left along it, with Orrit's Wood immediately left. Eventually swing slowly round to cross the bridge over a brook and join the Cheshire Lines Path in the scrub woodland on Shacklady's Heath. This section of the path is well used but permissive only.

The longer route continues along the barred lane over the railway bridge to meet the Cheshire Lines Path at the next bridge. Walk southeast along the path beside Downholland Moss Nature Reserve (which does not have open access) to meet the suggested route at the Shacklady's junction. Trains ran through here between Aintree and Southport from 1881 to 1952.

For the shorter route continue straight ahead through the village at the end of Riding Lane and out into the unfenced fields as far as the school. Take the path to the right on the nearside of Thorns Farm and, where this reaches an access track, turn right for 200 metres and then left along a path which reaches the Cheshire Lines Path at a three-arched stone bridge. Bear to the left to follow the suggested route.

From Shacklady's junction the Cheshire Lines Path continues in the Liverpool direction. From the new plantings of rowan and cherry cross the former heathland, with the tower of Aughton church standing out on Clieves Hills to your left. Go under the bridge of the B5195 and pass a sewage works on the right. Ignore the first two possible crossings of the large drain to your left and wait until you have passed the beech wood up to the left. An arrow to the left beside a new plantation of willow and alder (with Gore House farm buildings now in sight ahead along the path) indicates the turn up to Acres Lane. At the lane (which is the county boundary) cross over left and immediately right to walk up the rise of the field towards the wood on the brow with Our Lady's church, Lydiate, tucked behind it. The path is signed through to the A567 and passes the ruined tower of St Catherine's chapel on the right. Our Lady's RC church dates back to 1854 and St Catherine's to the 15th century; some of its contents have been transferred to Our Lady's. Follow the footway on the far side to the right and pass the thatched Scotch Piper pub to reach a path to the left on the far side of the canal bridge (Lollies Bridge). The name of the Scotch Piper was changed from the Royal Oak following the 1745 rising when a detachment of Bonnie Prince Charlie's soldiers left a wounded comrade here during their retreat. It is wooden cruck built and is claimed to be the oldest pub in Lancashire (though now just in Merseyside) – but see Walk 29.

In a short distance, a sandstone bridge leads back across the canal. Turn right along the towpath. This leads you direct to your start at the Ship.

15 **Slaidburn**
The Hark to Bounty Inn

Slaidburn village (the name perhaps signifying flat pastures amongst the ubiquitous hill slopes) is most attractive and draws visitors from a great distance. It was set up as the administrative centre of the former hunting forest by the de Lacy family in the last years of the 11th century. Deer were relatively soon restricted to defined areas, or 'parks', and much of the rest become cattle ranching land throughout the Middle Ages. The place has always been out of the way and this, combined with the need to enforce the forest laws, led to the establishment of the only court between York and Lancaster. For several hundred years it met in an upper room of the Hark to Bounty Inn and only ceased in 1937; the room now serves as an extension to the tearoom facilities during the summer and as a function room. The pub was earlier called the Dog but was renamed in 1895 when the local squire (also the parson) stopped for refreshment which was interrupted by the baying of the hound pack and prompted him to say 'Hark to Bounty', his favourite hound.

The rather squat range of buildings which forms the inn, just to the left of thc main junction in Slaidburn village, has been there since the 13th century – though not originally as a pub. Much of the inside of the building betrays the lack of stature of our ancestors and it can safely be described as both cosy and welcoming. Accommodation is surprisingly modest in price and is much in demand, so advance booking is recommended. Someone with an eye to history, tradition and fun has produced a wide and varied menu which is available between 12 noon and 2 pm and from 5 pm and 9 pm from Monday to Saturday and from 12 noon to 9 pm on Sundays. Teas are available each afternoon. As an ex-Yorkshire pub it is no surprise to find Yorkshire Pudding on the menu as a starter. You might like to follow on with a casserole of mixed game (rabbit, pheasant, and venison, for example), and finish off with apple pie. Pasta, steak and fish dishes also figure but vegetarians will have to choose from salads or sandwiches. Licensing hours are from 11 am to 11 pm (10.30 pm on Sundays). This is a Scottish & Newcastle house with its usual range of beers plus Matthew Brown mild (S&N now own the MB label) and Theakston Best Bitter and Old Peculier. Families are welcome and there is a small beer garden at the rear.

Telephone: 0200 446246.

How to get there: Use the B6478 either from Clitheroe, to the south, or from Long Preston at the junction of the A682 and the A65, to the north-east; Slaidburn village lies at about the halfway point of the road, approximately 10 miles from either start point. Alternative minor roads are signed through the Forest of Bowland or from Gisburn.

Parking: The landlords are quite used to people taking a walk as well as visiting the pub. Should the car park be crowded, there is alternative public parking beside the bridge over the river Hodder.

Length of the walk: 4 miles. Map: OS Landranger 103 Blackburn and Burnley (GR 711524).

Slaidburn village largely consists of terraces of warm, square-cut, unpretentious sandstone houses with their doorways opening directly on to the street. A few, including the pub itself, retain the external stone stairways to what was the hayloft. Some, close to the health centre, are dated 1763. Many have been modernised and refurbished and often have colourful hanging baskets of flowers. Newer additions to the village have been largely achieved without detracting from its appearance; the war memorial and the Victoria Jubilee fountain at the junction, or the little Elizabeth II Jubilee garden by the Croasdale bridge, for example. In the 19th century, Slaidburn was a centre for the catching of rabbits the skins of which were dried in the fields beside the Hodder and used for making 'beaver' hats.

The immediate surroundings are the pastures on the lower valley sides with a

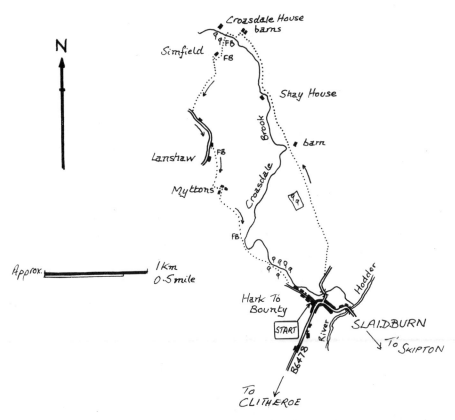

backdrop of moorland, largely kept for grouse shooting. Here and there, small woods and plantations break up the openness of the landscape and the Croasdale valley is a particularly quiet backwater with no motor road along the valley bottom.

The Walk

From the door of the Hark to Bounty turn left ten paces to the road junction. To visit the church and old grammar school go right in front of the youth hostel and then return. The late medieval St Andrew's church is most imposing and has a variety of interesting things inside it. Perhaps the best are the Georgian three-decker pulpit and the Jacobean screen. It still serves a massive parish of 75 square miles with barely 1,000 souls; there are far more sheep and cattle than people! Immediately next to the church stands the old grammar school, founded in 1717, and with a most attractively framed door.

Bear left as far as the war memorial and turn left down the brow to cross the bridge over the Croasdale brook. Walk round the bend of

67

the road to a stone stile over the wall on the left beyond the entrance of Townhead. Stay close to the right-hand boundary and climb up the field to a stile at the right-hand end of a shelter belt of beech and sycamore. The view back extends across the village and the middle reaches of the Hodder valley.

Cross the next field to a stone stile in the middle of the wall and the field beyond to a stile over a fence; the view is now up the Croasdale valley and to Dane Hill (with an ancient trackway running over it) and Fell End on either side. The third stile of this sequence leaves a small wood across the field to your left. Drop down now towards the bend of the river and a stone barn a little to the right. The path cuts across the bends of the river to reach the bridge across to the farm at Shay House. Continue beside the river over a further sequence of stiles to join the access track to Croasdale House and turn left along it. Just past some large, detached modern barns on the right the track does a double right-angle and in 50 yards you will find a footbridge to cross to the far bank of the river before you reach the house itself.

Walk up ahead through the small beech wood to a point of the fence left of a gateway. Use the stile and footbridge and cross between the fence and garden pond to come round the far side of the house at Simfield and join the access track. The view is now towards Pendle Hill and the whole of southern Bowland. Follow this track down to a lane and turn left. At the second barn turn left through the gate and bear half-right behind the agricultural implements of Lanshaw. Drop slightly to a stile and footbridge; it can be very wet here. Bear half-right again along the old hedge line on the far side of the field to a stile and cross two more fields to a stile into the yard at Myttons (where there is a craft shop selling pottery and other craftware – open only at weekends in the winter).

Cross the yard to the arrowed green lane between walls and follow the left-hand wall round to pass a gate on the left. Go through the gate at the end of the field and bear half-right down to a stone footbridge and stile; the woods of the narrow valley of the Croasdale brook are in view ahead. Walk along the left-hand boundary as close to the river as is practicable to pass below the remains of an old lime kiln beneath the farm buildings on the skyline up to your right. The path continues through the wood. This has been thinned out in recent times and shows a good growth of young ash. All along the river dippers search for water creatures. The path emerges on to a lane at the edge of the village. Turn left and go past the health centre back to the Hark to Bounty.

Bolton by Bowland
The Coach and Horses Inn

Bolton by Bowland lies at the extreme south-eastern corner of the Forest of Bowland and (as its name may mean) was once a much more important place than its aspect suggests today. The village is unusual (perhaps even unique in this area) in having two greens. The lower, and smaller, opposite the pub is marked by a cross and renovated stocks. The upper lies beyond the church and is edged by properties well built in the 19th century in Elizabethan and Jacobean style. Primrose Cottage, in Main Street, is dated 1716 and has an interesting decorated door lintel. A fine coach-house has been converted into an antique dealer's.

The Coach and Horses presents an imposing 17th century façade to the centre of the village street, almost opposite the smaller of the two greens and the sign for the Hellifield road. The spacious interior speaks of its days as a coaching inn and lends an expansive air which some pubs must envy. The menu here is changed frequently and is built around 'specials' which depend entirely on what is available as fresh produce in the local markets to make the genuinely home-made meals. A la carte is available at both lunchtime and in the evening, as are bar meals. When I last passed through, chicken breast with leeks

69

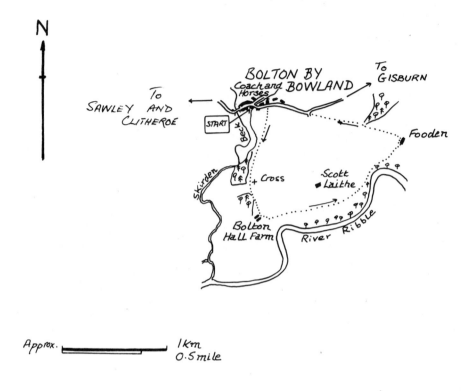

and Stilton cheese and baked ham with cream and cider made my mouth water. Food is served from 12 noon until 2 pm and from 7 pm to 9 pm (between 12 noon and 8 pm on Sundays and bank holidays). The best way, of course, of having the opportunity to sample both food and drink adequately would be to stay overnight.

A Whitbread house, the inn also serves Boddingtons and a guest beer and has Strongbow cider on draught. A more unusual speciality is a wide range of bottled lagers. There is also an extensive wine list. Bars are open from 11.30 am to 3 pm and from 6 pm to 11 pm. Families are more than welcome and the inn hopes to develop an area inside for them; meanwhile, the beer garden gives opportunity for the children to be happily occupied. Please ask before taking your dog into the bars.

Telephone: 0200 447202.

How to get there: From the A59 follow signs either via Sawley, east of Clitheroe, or from Gisburn village; about 4 miles in either case.

70

Parking: Plenty of parking is available behind the pub and adjacent to the village hall, and a small additional public car park is beside the new information centre next to the bridge over the Skirden beck at the western end of the village.

Length of the walk: 3 miles. Map: OS Landranger 103 Blackburn and Burnley (GR 785493).

The walk route links the village, the former hall and one of the many rather superior outlying farms, and gives good views all round from Pendle Hill to the lower Bowland fells. On the way, you will pass along the top of the Ribble gorge, upstream from Sawley.

A new information centre has been completed beside the bridge in 1993. Even if not manned, the noticeboards inside give details of other local walk routes and information about museums and events.

The Walk

Either first, or last, you may wish to complete the short walk through the whole village by proceeding west along Main Street down to the Skirden beck bridge and the information centre (which has adjacent public toilets).

Turn right from the pub entrance and cross Kirkbeck bridge and rise a little to the church of SS Peter and Paul. This church is 13th century with substantial 15th century remodelling but underwent extensive, but tasteful, rebuilding in the mid-19th century. The nave is long and low and bell openings exist at both levels of the fine tower. The Pudsay chapel and tombs date back to the late 1400s; quite a few of the other interior fittings are of detailed interest. Sir Ralph Pudsay had three wives and the number of children each bore (6, 2 and 17) is carved into the lower fold of the respective mother's gown on the tomb.

Assuming you have had a look inside the church, cross the churchyard direct to stone steps back down on to the road and take a few steps left before turning right up the driveway of Bolton Hall farm. Walk along the avenue of sycamore and oak with the Skirden beck across the parkland to your right. The way passes through new plantations and then rises up amongst scattered parkland trees. On the left, at the top of the brow and close to the start of a short walled section, stands the base of an old cross. The view is clear ahead to Pendle Hill. Drop down now towards a pillared gate of almost-red sandstone and bear round left with the track (ahead is marked 'private') and continue beside the wall to the buildings of Bolton Hall farm; 'Keeper's Cottage' is immediately in front of you. The buildings of Bolton Hall farm have seen some recent refurbishment after a

71

considerable period of neglect. The basis of the main building is of 1806 but the Pudsays were here for centuries before that. In 1464 King Henry VI took refuge here after the battle of Hexham (King Henry's Well is tucked away behind the hall). It has been suggested that the king (who spent nearly a year out of those regal duties here) may have been influential in deciding the present look of the church for it is not typical of this area. In later times, William Pudsay illegally extracted silver and minted coins but received pardon from Elizabeth I.

Take the track which turns round to the left and go up slightly to a path at the gate on the left. Cross the field to a stile and contour round the slope below the buildings of Scott Laithe using a series of three further stiles. Across to the right the isolated building standing out on the skyline is Dockber Laithe. At the gate, by the metal water trough, keep between the fences and pass a very fine lone field maple tree beside a second metal water trough. Continue to contour to meet the edge of the woods, with many dead elms standing out starkly, on the steep bank of the gorge of the river Ribble down below on your right. As the path works its way clearly along the top of the woods, there are occasional glimpses of the river below. Eventually it leaves the wood and crosses a field to the bottom of the yard of Fooden farm with its horned steers. The farmhouse is 17th century with a central two-storied porch.

Bear to the left around the buildings, following the signs, and cross a small field diagonally to the right to an arrowed stile. Gently climb up the next field to an up and over stile in the right-hand corner beside the end of a wood. Pendle is over your left shoulder now and the heather-covered fells around Beacon Hill, behind Grindleton, are ahead. Continue on the same line and drop slowly across two fields and walk along a row of youngish oak trees to exit on the Gisburn lane beside the entrance to Scott Laithe. Walk down the bank to the larger of the two greens beside the school and continue straight on to rejoin the start of the route at the church. Return to the Coach and Horses over the bridge.

17 Chipping
The Dog and Partridge Hotel

Chipping means a market or market town and it is clear that it served the immediate valley and the adjacent Hodder valley in the past, perhaps as an annual livestock fair rather than a weekly market. It continues to have a bustling air on sunny summer weekends. The stone cottages clustered about the church are an attractive picture, especially in Talbot Street and Windy Street. In the latter stands Brabins School, founded as a Bluecoat school in 1683.

The Dog and Partridge Hotel forms a significant part of the hamlet of Hesketh Lane, a little over a mile by road south of Chipping village. The long narrow sandstone building at the roadside has been there since 1515 though its current name replaced that of the Green Man relatively recently. The popularity of this pub has spread far and wide and it attracts a good trade at all times. Booking for full meals is probably wise at weekends. The menus for the bar, lunch and dinner are extensive. The policy is to offer largely traditional English food straightforwardly and substantially. I rather fancied the roast duckling or trout from the local trout farm, preceded by home-made soup, and followed by a wide choice of sweets and cheeses. (Fresh celery is used to set off the cheese – a delightful small touch.) A specials board is available each day also. Lunchtime service is from 12 noon until 1.30 pm (2 pm on Sundays) and dinner is served between 7 pm and 9 pm. On Saturday night and Sunday lunchtime meals are served in the dining-room only.

As a freehouse the Dog and Partridge serves a variety of real ales and keeps Tetley Dark Mild. The bar is open from 12 noon to 3 pm and 6.45 pm to 11 pm Monday to Saturday and to 10.30 pm on Sunday. The wine list is a full one. Families are welcomed at any time and there is a half menu available for the children. Dogs are not allowed in the pub.

Telephone: 0995 61201.

How to get there: Although it does not lie on any main road, Chipping is in the obvious embayment between the south-western fells of the Forest of Bowland and Longridge Fell and is signed from a wide distance around. The simplest approach is via Longridge or Clitheroe off the B6243.

Parking: There is a substantial car park at the pub but this may be crowded at weekends. An alternative is available by making the pub the halfway point of the walk and leaving the car in Chipping village at the large public car park behind the church.

Length of the walk: 4½ miles; the minor loop for Hesketh End adds no more than ¾ mile. Map: OS Landranger 103 Blackburn and Burnley (GR 619413).

The village lies slightly higher than the pub but there are no significant climbs along the way. The Chipping valley always seems to have a rich greenness about it at all times of year and has been pasture land for time out of mind. The view around of the enclosing heights runs from the isolated Beacon Fell (a Country Park about 3 miles away) through the snub peak of Parlick to the north, the wall of the Bowland Fells seemingly towering over the village, and round to the genuinely long ridge of Longridge Fell which delimits the southern skyline.

The area to the east of Chipping village was once one of the deer parks of Bowland, known as Leagram — the name still survives in that of the hall a mile north-east, and of the parish.

The Walk

Walk to the right from the pub doorway along the lane as far as Beech House. Take the stone steps to the right (there is no sign) and pass beside the house to a small field and cross to a steep up and over stile made of iron — obviously a local design which is found on many paths around. Drop down to the right to a white-painted gate and pass

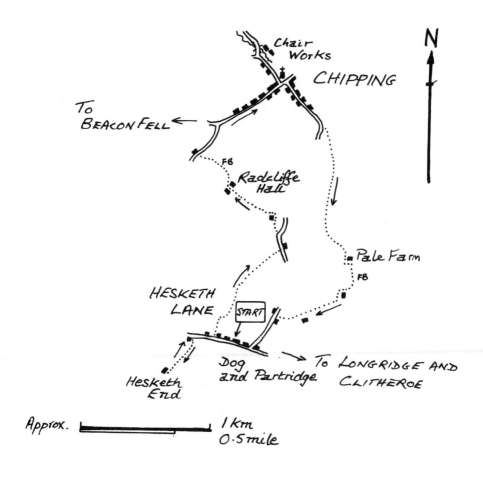

through it. Keep to the left-hand boundary as far as a stile and stone footbridge; the ground is rather wet here. The village church is clearly in view, with Parlick behind to the left, and Leagram Hall on a rise beyond the village to the right.

Cross the next field and pass by the buildings of Fields farm and follow a series of stiles to the road opposite Hardacre House. Turn left along the verge as far as the bend and continue straight ahead up the access track marked as a bridleway. In 100 yards turn left round Radcliffe Cottage and at the buildings of Radcliffe Hall swing right on a green lane to the gate at the top. Climb up the field and take the stile

75

through the hedge at the top of the brow and follow the stream up to Issac's Farm. Turn right along the lane and right at the road junction to enter the village and find the church to your left. The church of St Bartholemew certainly represents more than 700 years of continuity, and may well be the successor of a pre-Conquest Christian site. Like many others in the county, the outside is the result of Victorian restoration – though well done. Inside, it has retained an older atmosphere and some details may be 13th century; on one of the pillar capitals in the north aisle are carved four grimacing faces and the others have a variety of decorative motifs. A short diversion along the lane to the north and down the right fork to the river will take you to Berry's chair factory. A unique rural enterprise, it represents three generations of family effort and produces fine quality furniture in English hardwood. The cottages hard by were once the workhouse of Chipping. Return to the village centre and turn left to explore the road towards Clitheroe.

From the junction go down Windy Street and along to the bend at the bottom of the village. Take the path on the left over the stone bridge and immediately bear diagonally right across the field to pick up a track which gradually bends to the left to Pale Farm. This seems to derive its name from the 'pale', or fence, around the deer park and the route probably runs along the old boundary between the village and the farm.

Turn to the right along the far boundary of the field in front of the farmhouse and cross the footbridge in the corner. Move right of the next house and find a stile in the hedge and cross the access track to another. Cross a small field and turn right immediately you reach the far side of the hedge. At the access track to the next farm turn left but go ahead into the field in 50 yards instead of bending round towards the house. Take the stile on the right just before the telephone line and walk through to the road. Turn left along the far verge and walk back to the junction at Hesketh Lane. The pub is round the corner to the right.

Just beyond the first stile of the route, and on the far side of the lane, is a path, from the nearside of the brick house, which crosses four narrow fields to Hesketh End. The small additional walk is worth it to see the strange, curious and unique frieze in Latin which Richard Alston, who built the house in 1528, put in to describe the history of England. On the gable end of the large barn he enjoined 'O Lord, save it and be kind'. Return to the pub by the same route.

18 Waddington
The Higher Buck

The first part of Waddington's name may refer to either the ford of the river Ribble close to where Brungerley Bridge now stands, or to the low limestone knoll which overlooks it in the grounds of the present Waddow Hall. The present village, the 'tun', is set back from the potential flood plain of the river on either side of the beck which runs beside the main street. The memorial gardens and the efforts of householders along the street make this one of the most picturesque sights in Lancashire, especially from May to July.

Originally the Higher Buck was known as The Buck i' th' Vine, an allusion to the story of the patron saint of hunters, St Hubert (an 8th century bishop of Maastricht), who came upon a stag bearing a cross between its antlers. The pub got its present name to distinguish it from the other, and lower, 'Buck' which you will pass on the walk route. Its position is square-on to the street as you come up the rise from Clitheroe and at first it seems the building totally blocks off exit from the top of the village. It has done its customers good service since at least 1747. Overnight accommodation can be booked in advance. Lunchtime food is served between noon and 2 pm seven days a week. Food is available in the evening on Friday and Saturday only, from

7.30 pm to 9.30 pm. The offering is simple and plain, but good. Something of a speciality are the giant Yorkshire puddings and giant sausages. The chicken, ham and steak standards are complemented by chilli and a vegetarian selection. Hot roast beef sandwiches are popular snacks.

Real ale is a feature of the bar. Thwaites Bitter, Best Mild and Craftsman Premium are on draught; Carlsberg Export and Strongbow cider are also available. Drinking hours are 11.30 am until 3 pm and 7 pm to 11 pm on weekdays, 11 am to 11 pm on Saturday and 12 noon to 3 pm and 7 pm to 10.30 pm on Sundays. There is no garden area but tables are set out beside flowerbeds by the front door. An area inside accommodates families. Dogs are welcome, but please do check before taking them into the premises.

Telephone: 0200 23226.

How to get there: Use the B6478 (signed to Slaidburn) from the eastern end of Clitheroe. The pub is at the top end of the village.

Parking: There is a very large car park hidden round the back of the building and a very small amount of public parking is also available across the street.

Length of the walk: 3 miles; 5 miles if a detour into Clitheroe is included. Map: OS Landranger 103 Blackburn and Burnley (GR 728439).

One of the prettiest villages in the county is linked with the banks of the county's major river on this walk. There is also an option to visit Clitheroe, perhaps the finest market town in Lancashire. Waddington Hall is tucked away in the angle between the Clitheroe and West Bradford roads and not open to the public. It was from here that Henry VI fled the Yorkist men of the Talbots of Bashall in 1465 but was captured crossing the Ribble ford at Brungerley and sent to London, ignominiously tied facing to the rear, on the back of a mule.

The Walk
Start off straight from the door and walk down the street past the Methodist chapel on the right. If you have not already done so, you will want to take a closer look at the gardens beside the beck so cross over the first bridge and walk along 50 yards or so before returning to enter the Mitton road. A few paces along is St Helen's church. This is a medieval foundation rebuilt by the Victorians. Beside it are the old smithy, stocks and the pinfold for stray cattle and other animals. Having also had a look there, turn to the left outside the gate and keep left round the wall to pass the 'lower' Buck. This is owned by the almshouse trust and the rent contributes to keeping the 'hospital'

going. It is, itself, a listed building. In 100 yards the main road bears to the right. Keep straight ahead, however, beside a channeled stream dividing the gardens of several modern bungalows from the road and walk out of the village. The fields of Waddow Park open out to the left with small, scattered woods on a low limestone knoll, which obscures the hall from sight. Continue along the lane, past an isolated bungalow on the right and with the stub end of Longridge Fell in view in front. Fifty yards beyond the entrance to Fields farm, with its small caravan site, take the path to the left through the iron gate on the bend by a copse and pond.

The track leads round towards the hall and the path is signed round the left of the buildings and wall, on the slope of the knoll, to circuit to the entrance driveway. Waddow Hall is one of those Victorian country mansions for industrialists which almost came 'off the shelf'. This is the main camp for Guides throughout Lancashire and there have been many alterations and additions to the grounds. It is, none

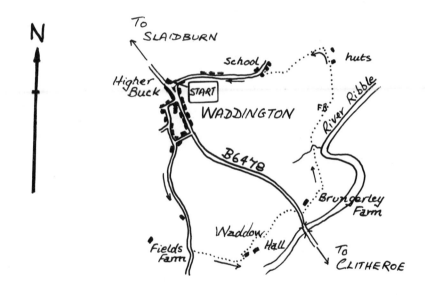

the less, a fine site up on the terrace of a former river level. On the river bank, Peg o' Nell's well is guarded by a headless stone figure said to represent a servant who fell on the slippery path when sent to fetch water for the hall, and died. Every seven years, Peg was reputed to claim the life of someone who was crossing the river. The parkland has many fine decorative trees and the squirrels are surprisingly tame – no doubt they are well used to the Guides. Bear right a little before the main gate to reach the B6478; the village of West Bradford is visible more or less dead ahead, the massive chimneys of the cement works are a little to the right, and a stretch of the river Ribble can be seen between. Opposite the buildings of Brungerley Farm, drop down the footway to the right by a quarry used as a road works depot, and cross over to an iron swing gate before you reach the bridge.

Immediately across Brungerley Bridge is the town of Clitheroe. An additional mile there, and another back, is well worth considering. This has been the centre of control for the Ribble valley since long before the Norman de Lacys built their castle, now a fine museum of local history and archaeology (open Easter to October), on its rock. The townscape is especially pleasing and a Town Trail is available from the information centre; telephone 0200 25566.

If you have made the diversion, retrace your steps to rejoin the main walk. The route follows the track below the farm buildings and can be very muddy where the cattle have churned it up as they climb up to the yard. After a short distance at river level, climb up on to a terrace and cut across the river bend along the left-hand boundary of the field and drop down again to cross the Waddington brook by an obvious farm bridge. Twenty yards on the right is a rather sagging stile which leads into a small enclosure and to a second farm bridge. The view behind now includes Clitheroe Castle as well as part of the town. Go ahead to a stile and flagged footbridge. In 50 yards, at a further stile, turn up the field to the left and aim for the stile at the top beside a shack, almost hidden amongst thorns and elder. Follow up the left-hand boundary, leaving a second shack across the field to your right, and use the iron gate. Stay close to the left-hand wall and go ahead over the next wall and aim for the bottom left corner of the next field past an oak tree; at this point there is an old wooden footpath sign. Bear half-right to a stile in the hedge behind the house gardens and walk between the huts to turn right across the yard to the road almost opposite the school. Follow the footway, to the left, back to the village and the pub past the gateway of the 'Hospital', which is all that remains of the original hospital, or almshouses, founded in 1700 by Robert Parker of Browsholme Hall; the rest is a tasteful modern remodelling.

80

Downham
The Assheton Arms

Downham village collects superlatives from its visitors, whether they are seeing it for the first time or are returning time and time again. The view down the street from beside the church, a little up from the Assheton Arms, is one of the finest in England (it has even been formally voted into the top half-dozen on one occasion). One or two other Lancashire villages come close in the attractiveness of their houses and layout but no other can have the unparalleled backdrop of Pendle Big End and that decides all. The fact that the village has been continuously under the control of the Assheton family (now the Lords Clitheroe) since the mid 1500s is the significant factor. They have exercised a restrained taste which is unbeatable; electricity cables, for example, were put underground here as long ago as the 1930s.

For nearly 400 years the Assheton Arms has stood at the top of the village and served many a passer-by. The building, of the local limestone, is externally in keeping with its neighbours and has the internal atmosphere which comes only with age and long occupancy. Its restaurant and function suite are justly famed. In the winter, the latter is used for dinner dances on Fridays and Saturdays, licensed until 1 am. Lunchtime service is from 12 noon until 2 pm and evening meals are served between 7 pm and 10 pm. The expected general range is complemented here by an unusually wide choice of fish and sea food – prawns piri piri, crab, salmon and plaice, for example. The surprisingly good taste of deep-fried soft cheeses is given a local flavour by mixing Lancashire cheese with Brie. Families are especially welcome and there is a special menu for the children. Menus are not printed but are varied on a daily basis.

Boddingtons, Flowers and Castle Eden beers are on draught in addition to the Whitbread beers of the house's own brewery. A variety of wines is on sale from the bar. Drinking times are from 12 noon until 3 pm and from 7 pm to 11 pm (10.30 pm on Sundays). Almost all the site is occupied by the buildings so there are no outside facilities. Well-controlled dogs are welcome but a check should be made at the bar before bringing them inside.

Telephone: 0200 41227.

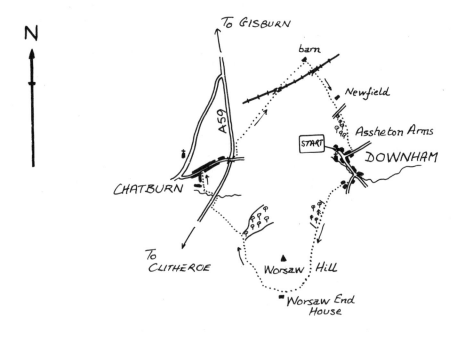

How to get there: Downham lies 4 miles north-east of Clitheroe. Approach from the A59, or from Clitheroe town, via Chatburn village. The pub is opposite the church.

Parking: Parking at the pub itself is extremely limited. Rather than occupy what there is unnecessarily, before going for your walk it might be better to leave the car in the spacious public car park beyond the bridge at the bottom of the street. (This car park has some of the county's – the world's perhaps? – most unusual toilets. Go and take a look for yourself.)

Length of the walk: 3 ½ miles. Map: OS Landranger 103 Blackburn and Burnley (GR 785442).

Downham's name is taken from its location amongst a group of small limestone hills which are the eroded remains of 300 million year old coral reefs. These have been extensively quarried within Chatburn parish, to the left of the route, and form the basis of the continuing cement production. The massive sandstone and shale bulk of Pendle Hill dominates the eye at first and the rich pastures and wildflowers of the limestone only get our attention with a closer look on foot.

The Walk

Start at the church opposite the pub. Only the tower of St Leonard's church is the original medieval construction; all the rest is a rebuilding of the early years of this century. Just behind it stands Downham Hall, the Tuscan-columned frontage of which is visible from the fields on the first part of the walk. In the bank at the bottom of the wall of the hall garden, to the left of the gates, just up from the church, is a stone which marks the grave of two Roman soldiers found when the wall was being constructed. Walk down the village street to the bridge over the Downham beck at the bottom and bear to the right as far as the entrance to the public car park. In front, between the two houses on the low brow, is a track which bisects the angle between the car park entrance and the lane to Worston. Follow this to a stile by the gate (there is no sign) and enter the field. Proceed along the right-hand hedge, past a fenced-off new planting on the left and Longlands Wood on the right, towards Worsaw Hill. In the next field, the path cuts across to drop to the bottom right-hand corner and then contours round the base of Worsaw Hill above the wall behind Worsaw End House. In season, the hedges will be alive with May blossom and roses. In front, now, is the snub end of Longridge Fell and, to its right, the easily recognisable top of Parlick, above Chipping.

Continue to contour round the hill inside the wall, passing several exposures of the reef limestone, until you have almost turned back on the original direction and you stand close to the corner of a beech wood. The cement works and the castle in Clitheroe are now to the left, the spire of Chatburn church is almost ahead, and the moorland of Waddington Fell lies beyond. Over the stile, drop steeply and with care down a small scar; the limestone can be very slippery underfoot when wet. The path continues straight down the fields to the edge of the A59, the Clitheroe bypass. Instead of climbing up the bank here, turn to the right between the fence and an old hedge line with a lovely field maple, to walk to the point at which the Heys brook flows under the road. On the left is a stile and a path up to the road edge. Cross the main road with great care – traffic is travelling fast at this point – and take the signed path down the far bank to the other end of the culvert. Three stiles in immediate succession put you on to the brook bank and a path which clings precariously to it for 100 yards and leads through to a track by the houses, with a footbridge on the left. Turn to the right and walk up to the Downham lane at Bould Croft past stone houses and cottages. Turn right up the footway to pass the police station on the other side of the road, and cross over the bypass bridge to the far end. Cross the road and take the path into the field at the bridge end.

An old grass track is clear along the left-hand boundary and Sawley village is visible ahead. Proceed along between hedges at the field end; the cattle churn this section up after wet weather. At the far gate bear to the left over a stone and iron bridge across the railway and turn right on the far side to continue on the old track beneath over-arching hedges for a while and then to the end of the field just short of a stone barn. Join a stone-surfaced track here and bear round, and down, to the right, to go back under the railway and climb up to the farm buildings at Newfield. Take the gate to the right of the house and cross up the field to a small green-painted iron gate on to the lane to Rimmington. Cross direct to an old stone squeeze stile and zigzag ahead up the brow of the field and take the track parallel to the wall of the wood on your right. At the far end, go ahead through the white gate by the cottages and walk down a short length of path between the walls of gardens to exit on the lane to Twiston. Turn to the right past the post office to return to the Assheton Arms.

20 Kelbrook
The Craven Heifer

Despite its Victorian public face, the village of Kelbrook has certainly been here at the junction of the valley pastures and the uplands since at least 1240. Little is left to indicate the older parts of the village except the rougher, lower, external appearance of the older cottages. Dotcliffe Mill, at the top of the road where you return to the village, is dated 1912 and is still operational. St Mary's church is of 1838 and has rather tall narrow windows.

The Craven Heifer is an extremely attractive and well-kept building on the western side of the road almost at the northern end of the village. The plain black and white frontage, with its offset porch, manages to look welcoming whatever the weather. Like many another Lancashire pub, it was undoubtedly once a farm and remains in, and of, the community in a way that many a more isolated inn can perhaps, sadly, no longer afford to do. The whole is summed up by being plain and simple, inside and out. The present policy is to serve meals in the bar at lunchtimes only. Mid-week service is between 12 noon and 1 pm and this is extended to 2 pm at weekends. Many another hostelry may pretend a more extended menu by attempting to provide 'added value' in words on paper. Here your roast ham, chicken or scampi are accompanied by good old Lancashire (or, perhaps one still ought to say, Yorkshire) chips. An equally straightforward sandwich board – beef, corned beef, ham, prawn and tuna – provides a satisfying snack for those who prefer not to walk on a full stomach. The children will find a burger to bring joy to their hearts. If you are carrying your own food, please do ask permission to eat it when buying your drinks.

The drinking hours are from 12 noon to 2 pm and 7 pm to 11 pm on weekdays, all day on Saturday, and from 12 noon to 3 pm and 7 pm to 10.30 pm on Sundays. Theakston's real ales and Blackthorn cider are both on draught. Although the pub does not cater specifically for children, families are welcome, as are well-controlled dogs.

Telephone: 0282 843431.

How to get there: Kelbrook is at the junction of the A56 Burnley to Skipton road with the B6383 from Barnoldswick. The pub is ¼ mile north of the junction.

Parking: The large car park is slightly detached from the pub, beyond the shop in the Burnley direction. There is additional parking along the terrace across the road.

Length of the walk: 3 ½ miles. Map: OS Landranger 103 Blackburn and Burnley (GR 901447).

The route of the walk overlooks the land of Craven (once almost a kingdom of its own), the broad valley which links Lancashire to Yorkshire through the Aire Gap. Kelbrook is one of a string of fairly unprepossessing small places, many of them now subsumed into larger names – like Burnley, Colne and Nelson – along the routes which make use of the lowest crossing of the Pennines, between the valley of the Lancashire Calder and the river Aire, in Yorkshire. The area of Craven, which also extends north into the upper Ribble valley, has a certain unity of landscape to it but the Yorkshire Dales National Park, to the north-east, and the moorlands which run southwards towards Rossendale, make for firm boundaries.

The valley of the Harden Brook shows a definite step just above Heads House and, beyond that point, the rushy fields are often wet and cold; maintaining good pasture here cannot be an easy job. The side of the valley you walk up on faces the sun and has been broken up into medium-sized fields over the years. On the return side the fields are much larger and above Thick Bank there remains a large area of heather and bilberry moor. Kelbrook Wood occupies the shadier side of the upper valley. Down by the village many of the fields are the sort of small crofts which are associated with families with more than one occupation – part-time small-holding, part-time in a mill.

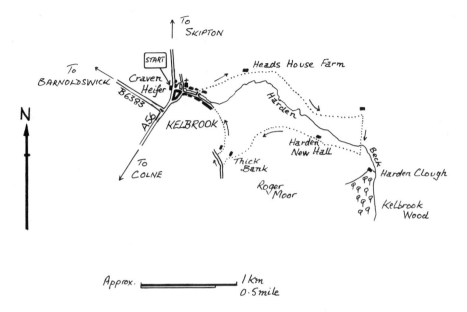

The Walk

Cross the main A56 in front of the pub with care and go along the short street of terraced houses opposite. At the far end are two bridges. Go over either of these into the road outside St Mary's church and make for the road in front of the cottages on the left alongside the Harden beck. In 50 yards, at the bridge from the right – which leads to Dotcliffe Road by the parish hall and opposite High Fold – go to the left up the brow along a bridleway. This is Heads Lane which is joined from the left by the Pendle Way in about ¼ mile. Follow the arrowed route ahead and past Heads House farm to go along a track lined with rowan, holly, thorn and gorse, to a field gate. Just beyond this is the circular mound of a covered reservoir on your right. The view behind now extends over much of the area known as Craven, on the Lancashire-Yorkshire border.

Keep beside the left-hand boundary to an up-and-over stile followed by a small stream and a second similar stile. The path bends slightly to the left and passes another Pendle Way sign. Continue over two further fields to the left-hand corner behind the farm at Harden Old House. Turn right along the inside of a double fence with a young hedge planted in between and drop to an up-and-over stile at the wall, partly hidden behind the fences. On the far side, go down to the Harden beck and look for a convenient point at which you can reduce a leap to a stride. Up to your left, Kelbrook Wood occupies the

87

western slope of the right-hand fork of the valley. Rise a little in 50 yards to the nearest telegraph pole. Turn right to a gateway and head for the buildings at Harden New Hall. Pass the sign bearing white arrows and join the access track. The route continues along this, contouring round the slope of the hill below Roger Moor to reach Cob Lane beside the farm at Thick Bank (where there is a small flock of Jacob sheep). Turn to the right and go down the lane past the entrance of a small quarry, used as a base by a company which cleans stone buildings by sandblasting them, and turn into the next track on the right following the signed path along it. In 20 yards you will pass the entrance gate of a barn conversion. Continue ahead to the field gate and go through the wicket gate immediately to the left into the garden and pass behind the building to a stile.

Drop down the left-hand boundary to a wicket and then a stile in the angle of the wall. Once over the stile stay on the right-hand boundary on an obvious path line and walk down the slope through a gap in old walls to reach a stone squeeze stile by a gate and holly tree by the houses. This is the top of Dotcliffe Road; continue ahead to rejoin the route from the pub by the two bridges and church. Turn back along the terrace to the Craven Heifer.

If you would like to add to your excursion, close by, and easily visited before or after the walk, are two interesting museums. At the northern end of the next village, Earby, in the old grammar school building, is the Dales Mining Museum. Opening times are quite constrained, so it is wise to telephone beforehand (0282 843210). Across the valley is the town of Barnoldswick with Bancroft Mill (telephone 0282 842214) where a steam engine which, in its time, drove 1,250 looms, can be seen in action.

21 Brierfield (Worsthorne)
The Roggerham Gate

Roggerham is a small hamlet with no church, chapel or shop. Nowadays, folk refer to it most often by the name of the pub into which all its essence seems to have been distilled. The derivation of the unusual name is uncertain. An inn has stood here since at least 1674 but it seems likely that the name of the hamlet is much older than that. Two possibilities, equally plausible, are that it is either a link back to Norman times, when Roger of Lancaster, and then Roger de Lacy, held the Forest of Blackburnshire from the King, or that it was, simply, the hide-out of a band of robbers. Certainly, this is an obvious 'gateway' to the moorland of Rossendale and is much used by walkers.

Although in recent years the sign has not hung over the doorway, the Roggerham Gate is one of those inns which used to display the words:

> This gate hangs free and hinders none;
> Refresh and pay and travel on.

The present landlord is very keen to re-establish a reputation for good service far and wide. The building stands halfway up a hill and presents a very different aspect depending upon your angle of approach. Don't be misled. Once inside you will find it light and airy though still comfortably cosy. Food is available at lunchtimes between 12 noon and 2 pm and in the evening from 7.30 pm until 10.30 pm (10 pm on Sundays). There is a small dining-room, in addition to the bar, and the inn has a supper licence. The menu has a good variety, including some of the commoner 'exotic' dishes (like chicken tikka and chilli con carne), but – I am told – it is the gammon that folk from round about regard as worth travelling especially for. Baked potatoes with a variety of fillings, salads and sandwiches are served for the lighter eater. If you prefer the traditional mill-town pie and peas you can get it here. An unusual feature is the selection of teas offered.

This is a Younger pub with IPA, No. 3, and Scotch Bitter on draught, plus Theakston. The bar is open from 11 am to 11 pm through the week; at weekends it opens at 12 noon, and closes at 10.30 pm on Sunday. Families are more than welcome everywhere in the pub. Please check at the bar before walking in with your dog. Saturday evenings are live-music events and well patronised.

Telephone: 0282 422039.

How to get there: From the A56 either turn for Worsthorne at the crossroads by Brierfield station or, from the roundabout at the eastern end of Burnley, follow signs for the Burnley Football Club ground and then look for the left turn for Worsthorne. Roggerham Gate is 1½ miles north of Worsthorne village centre, just over the boundary into Brierfield.

Parking: Substantial parking is available behind and below the pub; please check at the bar before going for your walk.

Length of the walk: 3 miles. Map: OS Landranger 103 Blackburn and Burnley (GR 882337).

The walk route explores the edge of these exposed uplands – if they ever did have many trees on them, they are long gone, chopped or chewed. (I was forcibly reminded, on a late summer's day, that driving, cold rain can be on you in minutes out of a seemingly clear sky over the shoulder of Boulsworth Hill – 'wuthering' is certainly, as Emily Brontë said, an apt adjective.) Some of the farms are still functional but more and more the outlying barns have been abandoned and many of the buildings renovated to become retirement and commuter homes. Evidence that our ancestors were here well before Roman times is the burial mound on Pike Lowe; perhaps those were warmer days. Up above Holden Clough, on the right, is an earthwork known as Twist Castle. Many prehistoric worked flints have been found in the area too, scattered beside the old trackways. We still have our long-distance routes across these moors; the Brontë Way, to Howarth, begins near here.

The Walk

Walk up the lane from the front of the pub and pass a stone drinking trough to reach an access track to the right. Turn along this and continue to the near side of the garden fence of the nearest building (a new one) at Ing Hey. Turn to the left in the field and work your way round the outside of the garden and down to a gap in the wall at a stream. Find a way across the muddy patch and go left along the far side of the wall to an old stone squeeze stile. Bear slightly up to the right now towards a stone barn and, at the far end of it, drop to cross the stream of Holden Clough and climb up to the wall. An up-and-over stile leads you to a track on the far side; turn to the left. Follow the track back across the valley, leaving some new planting of trees away to your right, and rise up the side to pass beside the buildings of Sweet Well House. At the top of the brow the view is almost 360°: Rossendale to the south, Pendle north-west, Ingleborough and Penyghent to the north-east.

Use the access road and go down past the tumulus on Pike Lowe on

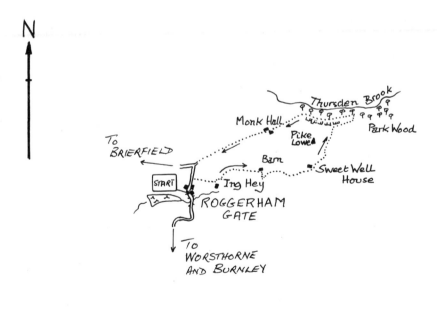

your left to an up-and-over stile (with a Brontë Way sign on it) straight ahead at the lower bend. Move ahead to a signed post and then bear to the right to drop down the side of the Thursden valley through old stone quarry workings. The view up past the woodlands around the house at Thursden to Boulsworth Hill is most attractive. Cross a broken wall and go steeply down to a stile. Ignore this and turn hard left, back up the slope, on a narrow path taking a more gentle line, through the woodland of oak, birch, sycamore, rowan and alder to cross the bottom of the quarried area. At the far end follow the sign and use the gate by the sheep pens. Proceed along the grassy track to the buildings of Monks Hall and walk between them. Monks Hall was once a grange of the Abbey of Kirkstall, near Leeds. The lovingly restored building (now a house) shows its considerable age but nothing specific, so the owner told me, dates it before the dissolution of the abbey in the 1530s. The remains of fishponds are still to be seen down beside the Thursden brook. The monks won coal from the exposed seams up on the moor, and operated a mill on the Swinden beck, somewhere near the bridge below the pub. No doubt their main occupation here was sheep farming and it still remains the main agricultural use for the area.

Use the stile ahead at the far end of the main building and cut across the corner of the field to a second stile which takes you into the lane. Turn to the right down this to the junction with the Brierfield road at the bend. Return to the Roggerham Gate by walking left down the hill watching out for traffic.

Above and below the pub the valley of the Swinden beck has been dammed for reservoirs. In past times, the Extwistle Mill stood near the lower one and provided employment for the people of Worsthorne.

Hurst Green
The Shireburn Arms Hotel

The buildings which now form the 16-bedroom Shireburn Arms Hotel were part of the Stonyhurst estate when built in 1679; today the hotel often serves those who have occasion to visit Stonyhurst College as well as the many passers-by who visit the village and the college grounds. It faces up the village street, across the attractive small green and forms an equally engaging backdrop, with its creeper-clad walls, when looking towards it from the opposite direction. Food is served in the lounge bar from 9.30 am to 9.30 pm with the hot food menu available from 12 noon to 2.30 pm and from 5 pm to 9.30 pm; coffee and tea are served throughout the day. The Valley restaurant opens Monday to Friday from 12 noon to 2.30 pm and on Sundays from 12 noon until 6 pm. The evening menu is served from 7 pm to 9.30 pm. The à la carte menu offers a gourmet choice – mussel and cider soup, perhaps, followed by poached salmon with saffron lobster sauce, fresh sweets, English and Continental cheeses, and coffee with petits fours.

The lounge bar is open all day for cask ales and also foreign beers; the hotel is a freehouse. Ciders and stouts are available on draught. The wine list runs to nearly five dozen items so there should be something to suit your taste and mood. Families are welcomed throughout the hotel. Please ask at the bar is you wish to eat your own food on the patio with your drinks (at the time of writing, there were plans to open facilities aimed towards the passing walker). The age of the hotel means that the inside does not cope well with the larger breeds of dog, but small breeds are welcome; please remember to check at the bar first.

Telephone: 0524 826518.

How to get there: In the centre of the village of Hurst Green, on the B6243, halfway between Longridge and Clitheroe. Alternatively, use the B6246 from Whalley town centre.

Parking: There is a restricted amount of parking in front of the hotel and a bigger car park round the back at the eastern end. You will be welcome to use the car park while going for a walk, but please notify reception that you are doing so. Additional car parking will be found along the village street on the far side of the green.

Length of the walk: 3½ miles. Map: OS Landranger 103 Blackburn and Burnley (GR 685379).

A pleasant river valley walk with wider views than usual and with no difficult slopes to negotiate. It is particularly enjoyable in the height of summer and on a sunny, crisp day in winter. The village is a quiet corner now – except for tourists – but the Dean, running by on the western side, was another of the many sites of early industry which has now returned to nature – once there were four mills here. The Ribble Way, which this walk follows for a short distance, is a Long Distance Path jointly sponsored by Lancashire and North Yorkshire County Councils, and the Yorkshire Dales National Park. It starts by the marshes where the Douglas meets the Ribble at Longton and ends at Gavel Gap, above Ribble Head. A descriptive booklet is available from information centres.

The Walk

Take the footpath left (east) of the hotel buildings and pass between the petrol station and the rear car park to a stile at the bottom marked for the 'Ribble Way'. The view ahead is of the chimneys of Langho Hospital across the river, the ridge from Whalley to Blackburn, and through the gap at Whalley, beyond Pendle to Padiham. Aim down the field towards the chimneys, pass the water trough at Parker's Well, and cross to the right of the stream about 50 yards further on, where there is a small sign. Drop down yet further, between two streams lined with oak and alder, until you reach two stiles into Raid Deep woods on the bank of the river Ribble (the woods are the 'hursts'

94

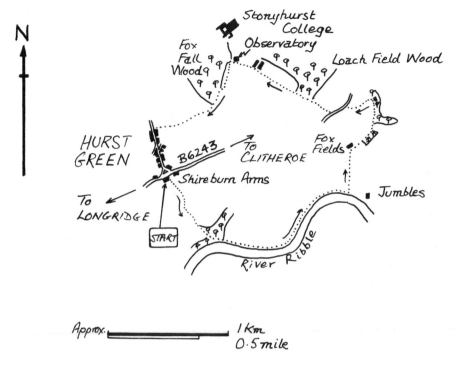

N

HURST
GREEN

To
LONGRIDGE

Stonyhurst College
Observatory
Fox Fall Wood
Loach Field Wood
B6243
To CLITHEROE
Shireburn Arms
Fox Fields
Jumbles
START
River Ribble

Approx. |⎯⎯⎯⎯⎯⎯⎯| 1 Km
0·5 mile

which give the name to both the village and the college). Descend through the wood and exit at the eastern side over a footbridge. Stay beside the river bank to the aqueduct; Dinckley Hall is on the far bank at this point. The river is slow and limpid here with banks of Himalayan balsam and thistles in summer and the occasional silent fisherman; sand martins hawk for insects over the water.

Continue along the bank beside the fields (sometimes of maize, taller than you) as far as the shallows which form riffles in the water at the start of Jumbles bend. Walk gradually round the curve to where the rocks form a small cascade just short of the house at Jumbles. Notice the cross, up on the small hill over your left shoulder, which was moved here from the road that lies up and behind it; the Nick of Pendle will be clearly visible a little to your right. Cross up the track over the field to the left towards the buildings of Fox Fields but bear right along the access track before you reach them and pass the orchard hedge. Walk on into a shallow valley, past a recent plantation of Scots pine and spruce on the right, until you reach a stone cottage on the right-hand side. Turn to the left through the gate opposite (there is no sign) and go up the left-hand field boundary to the B6243.

Proceed left along the footway for 100 metres and cross the road to the footpath.

Rise gently up along the side of Loach Wood and go along the side of the buildings at Hall Barns to a green iron gate in the corner by the wood just beyond the domed observatory. Immediately before this is a view towards Stonyhurst College buildings, through the gate which is used as access to the playing fields on your left. Stonyhurst College is a Jesuit foundation, which came here in 1794. The frontage is very imposing and the observatory is unique. There have been many additions since Sir Richard Shireburn created the basis of the buildings in 1592. The formal gardens and two parallel canals were built just over a century later by Henry Wise, gardener to King James II. Cromwell spent the night here before his success at the battle of Preston. Wise was also responsible for the almshouses which were transferred to their present site in the village in 1936 from Kemple End on Longridge Fell – they are now homes for workmen on the estate. The Hall Barns farm buildings contain large cruck-trusses inside – unfortunately not generally open to view. The College buildings are open at weekends in the summer (telephone 0254 826345 to check arrangements).

Move gradually right to the wood edge and drop down over the stream more or less opposite the brick pavilion. A series of four iron kissing-gates leads through in a straight line to the top of the village along Smithy Row beside the bowling green. Turn left in front of the almshouses and pass the Bailey Arms to return to the Shireburn Arms.

23 Love Clough
The Huntsman

Love Clough appears to mean wet or boggy clough; Goodshaw – the next village – almost certainly derives from a woman's name associated with a wood. The Huntsman is where the local Round Table holds its meetings, so you can be sure of a good welcome. The Ordnance Survey believes Love Clough is a two-word name, but the locals seem to prefer to use one; either way, there cannot be many pubs with a road number of 1222 in its address! Locally the place is known as the Glory because Baptist revival meetings used to be regularly held in the field behind. The building of the Huntsman is good 19th century four-square sandstone and, like its neighbours, puts its better face to the road. Bar food is served throughout the week between 12 noon and 2.30 pm. The restaurant is open from 5.30 pm until 8 pm on Thursday, to 10 pm on Friday, and from 7 pm to 10 pm on Saturday. Meals are available from 12 noon until 7 pm on Sundays. The emphasis is on home cooking so that the chicken and mushroom pie, steak and kidney pie, and the chicken and beef curries are not from multi-store freezers but good home-made fare with local ingredients. The specials board includes a vegetarian offering. Sandwiches, snacks and jacket potatoes with fillings provide an extensive bar choice. Children's portions are available.

The current beers at this freehouse are John Smith's, Webster's Yorkshire Bitter and Wilson's Original Mild, and lager and Guinness are also on draught. At the time of writing, there is no special area for families but the intention is to develop a beer garden. Please ask before bringing your dog into the comfortable, open-fired taproom.

Telephone: 0706 213779.

How to get there: About 2 miles south of the crest of the A682, Burnley to Rawtenstall road on the right-hand side, at the northern end of the village.

Parking: The car park lies north of, and below, the pub. Permission will gladly be given to leave your car while you walk.

Length of the walk: 3 miles. Map: OS Landranger 103 Blackburn and Burnley (GR 811272).

The valley forms a great open bowl on the western side, opposite Love Clough, and the walk ascends the upper side of this and circuits along the ridge to give a glimpse down the other side to Accrington, and wider views all round.

Grazing land extends all the way up to the tops in this part of Rossendale. The medieval forest had been steadily encroached on over several hundred years but there was a considerable extension as the climate warmed in the late 17th century to reuse land which our prehistoric ancestors seemed to have cleared and colonised in the last century BC.

The valley is one of four which run north to south into the main Rossendale valley of the river Irwell out of what was once the Forest of Rossendale. Layers of hard millstone grit are interspersed with softer shales and produce the characteristic stepped outlines of the upper valley sides. In amongst them are beds of coal and the lodge which can be seen in the lower part of the second clough (Great Clough) served Goodshaw Hill colliery, which closed in 1934. Dunnockshaw, just up the valley beyond the plantation, was the base for lead mines in the late 1700s (lead is a metal rarely found in such rocks), some of which were in the first clough (Whin Hill Clough) beside which you climb up to the ridge. More recent developments are the many reservoirs: Mitchell's House reservoirs were built to serve Accrington between 1855 and 1876.

The Walk

Leave the pub entrance to the right and walk along the footway to the corner of Commercial Street and turn right down the hill (along part of the Rossendale Way) and pass the terraces to reach the bridge over the Limy Water amongst the buildings now labelled 'Love Clough Country Business Park' – a conversion of the former mill buildings.

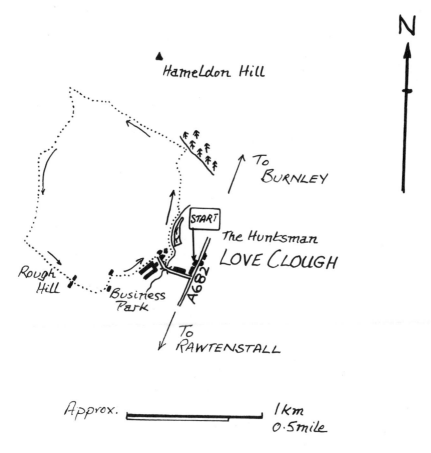

Over the bridge go right before the old stone building of the Social Club, dating back to the 1700s, and walk upstream past some new houses behind – but which have old stone re-used in their facing. Keep ahead on the arrowed path beside the concrete leet with its weirs and the lodges, which formerly fed the works, on the far side. After 250 yards bear to the left between the broken wall and the thorn hedge and take the track right and straight past the large iron post by a gap on your right. The track gradually lifts up a pasture to the edge of a large plantation of larch, pine, spruce and sycamore. The view back extends down the valley to the tops around Cowpe Low, beyond Rawtenstall.

Take the gate to the left and climb the field outside the plantation keeping to the left of the telephone line. The masts of the weather station on Hameldon Hill are clear on the skyline. Aim for the point where the wall ahead just nicks the skyline and walk up an angled path and through a gap. Bear round to the left up the top of the clough where there is a stile at the junction of the walls. On the top you will be able to see south to Holcombe Tower and round, through Winter Hill, to Darwen Tower to the west. The immediate area has been churned up in recent times by competitions for four-track vehicles and this has obscured the path. The simplest thing to do is to follow the left-hand edge of this area and work up the wall line to a gate on a track. Go left through this and pick up an arrowed route labelled 'Round the Hill' (joining part of the Rossendale Way once more) at the next gate, on the far side of the clough from the four-track area.

Follow the clear track along broad ridge between tumbled walls; it can be extremely wet underfoot through this section. On a clear day, it is possible to make out, half-right of you, the gas holder at Southport, on the west coast. At the gate, where the walls end, continue ahead along the wall to the right until you reach a dog-leg in the wall. A stile takes the path, on the same line, to the far side of the wall – Mitchell's House reservoirs and the town of Accrington lie down to the right. Between the first wall joining from the left and the second such wall, there is an obscure stone stile (be careful of the wire stretched against the top of it) to a path which goes down slope. Edge towards the left-hand boundary and descend steeply amongst eroded gullies to a stile at the left of the back of the house at Rough Hill.

Cross the yard and pick up the track downhill. Stay with this to pass a house on the right at a bend, and a second on the left, also at a bend, and arrive at the back of the works buildings which are now the Business Park. Follow round to the bridge and go back to the Huntsman up Commercial Street. The works at the bottom of Commercial Street were a print works belonging to Messrs Cooke and Unsworth and were supplied with coal from the colliery up the hill.

24 Belthorn
The Dog Inn

Belthorn is a single street of houses of varying ages with no pretentions to beauty. The sandstone pub is, by far, one of the best of the buildings but undated, so far as I can tell. The Dog sits right on the boundary between the districts of Blackburn and Hyndburn and has a reputation which extends far beyond both. Though the wind always seems to blow across this ridge, the warm and welcoming interior will complement both adverse and serene weather outside. Food, both à la carte and table d'hôte, is available in the restaurant and meals and snacks are served in the bar. Service is from 12 noon until 2 pm and from 7 pm to 10 pm and all day on Sunday until 9 pm. The menu is very extensive, with a wide international range; the pub even offers to prepare anything you prefer – provided the ingredients are to hand and you are willing to wait. Picking out anything only leaves you wishing you had the space for something else. How about starting with something from the sea – a simple smokies salad, say, and following with steak with your own choice from one of no less than six different sauces, and ending with profiteroles? The combinations seem almost infinite. Vegetarians will also find a special of the day, as well as chow-mein and moussaka.

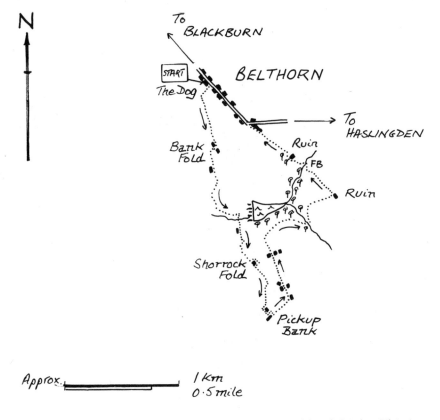

This wealth on the platter is matched by a wealth of drinks. This is a Whitbread house, with Boddingtons Bitter and Mild always on draught, together with guest beers, which might be Pompey Royal, Marston's Pedigree and Timothy Taylor Landlord. The stout is Murphy's and the lager both Stella Artois and Heineken. There are on-tap wines from Germany, Australia and California. Licensing hours are from 11.30 am to 3.30 pm and from 6.30 pm to 11.30 pm. Families are welcome at any time and there is a room allocated for their use. Please ask before bringing your own dog in – the resident model for the sign needs to give approval.

Telephone: 0254 690794.

How to get there: Use the B6231 from either Lower Darwen or Accrington, or the B6232 from Blackburn past Queen's Hospital. At Guide continue on the B6232 for ½ mile and bear off right to Belthorn village. The Dog is on the right at the lower end of the street.

Parking: There is plenty of parking space at the pub which walkers are welcome to use.

Length of the walk: 4 miles. Map: OS Landranger 103 Blackburn and Burnley (GR 716247).

This route explores the eastern slopes of the side valley of the river Darwen, which was once Hod's valley. It is full of evidence of the past without, it seems, ever having been in the centre of anything very much. The sunny side of the valley is yet another which betrays its greater richness by the smallness of the pasture fields and the greater scattering of buildings on that side. Bank and Shorrock Fold have both been there since a time when cattle keeping was indicated by the designation 'fold', and the 'stone hedges' could well have been put up then. Below lie the spoils of the former colliery and Hoddlesden, across the valley is effectively an outlier of the mills of Darwen.

Many properties have been modernised and had double glazing and central heating put in. Our ancestors – not so long ago – would have regarded all this as 'reet nesh'. From these wind-swept heights came bare-knuckle fighters and rough gamblers, cockfighters and illicit whisky makers. Self-taught educators, like Jeremy Hunt of Pickup Bank, taught others to read and write and perhaps, who knows, sowed the seed which eventually took most of the population away to what seemed more congenial spots.

The Walk

The route begins immediately along the upper side of the front car park (there is no sign), and goes past the row of cottages at right-angles to the road, to a stile hidden round the far end. Cross the first small field and take the stile to the left halfway along the left-hand boundary of the second field. The views, across to Darwen Tower and round through Hoghton to the fells of Bowland, are wide; as you turn the whole of the Hoddlesden valley is in sight. Move forward easily along the contour by a wall and old track to the buildings at Bank Fold. Keep left and then turn right down the track by the gates with lions on the posts. Follow the track round and past some houses and then under the power line and drop down over some old spoil heaps to the track by the stream in the clough.

Turn up to the left towards the dam and take the stile to the right immediately in front of the spillway. The path goes steeply up to the left-hand side of the cottage on the brow; on the way you pass the remains of an isolated old chimney to the right. Go ahead on the access track and round a modern barn to a gate. Go left and contour along to Shorrock Fold. Work your way round two sides of the buildings to a stile to the right beyond the small aviary in the corner of the garden. Walk down the edge of the garden and use the stile to the left immediately in front of the bottom wall. Follow the remains of this to the second field boundary and go through the fence (there is no stile) and cross the track to the stile opposite. Several lengths of stone flag fences will be in view. Aim towards the black and white building ahead and down to the right and cross the field to a crude stile about 20 yards up from the bottom right-hand corner. Drop to the right, through a gateway and walk round the fence on the left and along the garden of a house to a stile in the corner. Go immediately left and then right to the upper end of the buildings of the Old Rosins Inn at Pickup Bank.

Turn up the lane to the left and follow it round to the left between the houses until you reach a T-junction. Use the stile two paces to the left ahead and walk up the side of a horse jumping practice area and use a squeeze stile to move towards a row of three houses. The path goes between the bottom two and over a stile by the garage. Follow the right-hand boundary on an old track line to a decrepit stile in the right-hand corner. Trace the old wall line as far as the fence at the top of the wood and bear round it to the right to contour round Shooter's Hill and into the right-hand arm of the clough. A stile to the left leads you to a path down to cross the stream on flat beds of sandstone; to the left you can hear, but not see, a waterfall. Climb steeply up the far bank to a stile over the fence and aim left of the pylon to climb up to an old wall where it does a dog-leg. Cross the wall and walk through a rushy area, where snipe nest, towards the next nearest pylon. The ruins of a farm will become obvious. At these, turn to the left and aim towards Belthorn on the top of the hill. Stay high enough to avoid the very wet runnel and then drop down the telephone line to the edge of the other arm of the clough. Go steeply down the bank to a stone flag footbridge. From the fence on the far side you will be able to look down on to a second waterfall. The path climbs up to an oak tree and then to some more ruins. Walk up through the sycamore trees behind these to a stile by the gate on the right. On the far side of this, turn to the left along a track which reaches the top of the village past the row of cottages called Tower View. Walk down the street on the footway to return to the start opposite Chas Hooper's Drum Shop.

25 **Withnell**
The Hoghton Arms

Passing traffic has always been the lifeblood of the Hoghton Arms. A building of more than usual character, it has stood at the intersection of main roads since 1700; the village itself is some two miles distant. The inside has been modernised on more than one occasion, but retains an old world atmosphere and its generous space is subdivided in a most comfortable way. Bar and restaurant food is served, Monday to Friday, from 12 noon to 2.30 pm and from 5.30 pm to 9.30 pm. On Saturday service is between 12 noon and 9.45 pm, while on Sunday service ends at 9.30 pm. The present landlord has family connections with a fishmonger so the extensive menu includes, perhaps, the best choice of fish in the county. Nowhere else have I come across sole, plaice, halibut, haddock, salmon and scampi all on the same menu – and all of it fresh. If you wish to go wholly for fruits of the sea, your starter could be a seafood crêpe with lobster sauce. The commoner choices – steaks, chicken, pork, gammon and duckling – are not neglected and the vegetarian choice includes a rogan josh which you are unlikely to find too often. Lighter meals are available in the bar as well as sandwiches and salads. A special senior citizens' lunch is available on Thursdays. Should you fancy starting with breakfast (or taking it after an early morning walk) this is served from 10 am. The menus are changed in detail every six months or so.

Burtonwood brews, including James Forshaw's Bitter and Top Hat, are on offer, plus Stella Artois, Carlsberg and Castlemaine lagers, and Strongbow cider. The bar is open from 11 am to 11 pm throughout the week, and from 12 noon to 3 pm and 7 pm to 10.30 pm on Sundays. Part of the pub is set aside as non-smoking. As well as the beer garden there is an activity course of considerable complexity for the children. Only guide dogs are permitted inside.

Telephone: 0254 201083.

How to get there: On the southern side of the roundabout at the crossing of the A675, Bolton to Preston, and the A674, Blackburn to Chorley, roads.

Parking: There is extensive parking at the pub, which you will be welcome to use.

Length of the walk: 3 ½ miles. Map: OS Landranger 103 Blackburn and Burnley (GR 629243).

As a parish, Withnell (the hill of the willows) stretches from the high moorland of the West Pennines, at over 350 metres, down the western side of the Roddlesworth valley to the confluence of that river with the river Darwen at Feniscowles. Our walk takes in the lower part only, with very little height rise.

The short part of the walk along the edge of Roddlesworth Woods is beside what is now the largest remaining tract of broadleaf woodland in the county. It exends up the valley for several miles and it is possible to turn right on the path and make your way up beside the Roddlesworth reservoirs and to Tockholes.

This section of the Leeds and Liverpool Canal is entirely on one level. It meanders in gentle curves along the contour, thus providing varying views across the valley.

The final few hundred metres follow what is, clearly, an old drove-way. These had to be wide between boundaries to allow the cattle to pass and to feed along the way. When the field enclosures were made, many such routes became access ways to groups of fields, as it seems this one has. Because they do not generally provide much in the way of grazing they also, often, became narrow strips of woodland.

The Walk

Leave the front of the pub along the grass verge of the A674 in the Chorley direction and walk up to the bend on the brow by Ivy Cottage. Immediately beyond, take the footpath to the left and cross the field to another stile. Swing slightly uphill towards the wall end and take the stile just below it and then move along the side of the wall to the gate on to the A675. Take great care of traffic coming round the

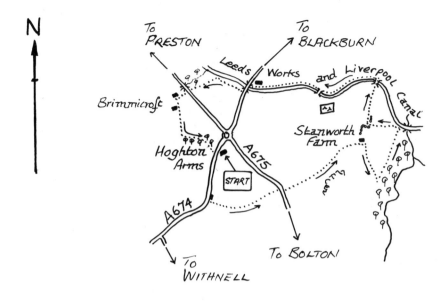

N

To PRESTON
To BLACKBURN
Leeds Works and Liverpool Canal
Brinnicroft
Stanworth Farm
Hoghton Arms
A675
START
A674
To BOLTON
To WITHNELL

Approx. |_____| 1 km
0·5 mile

corner from the left as you cross over the road to the access track of Stanworth Farm. Follow this beside the spoil heaps of the still-working Withnell Quarries on the right. At the farm gate is a small area of spoil recolonised by heather. Drop down slightly, towards the farm buildings, and with the view towards Hoghton Tower half left.

The locality has been dominated, in the past, by the de Hoghtons of Hoghton Tower (hidden by the woods on the hill to the north) and the pub bears their arms as its sign. The tower was quite late in being started, and overlong in its building – it took some 50 years from 1560. Here in 1611 King James I knighted the loin of beef during his visit to what was a newly finished house. The house was left unused for much of the 18th century and had to be substantially restored when the family moved back in the 19th. It is close enough to consider visiting when you come for the walk; opening times are basically on summer weekends but subject to change (telephone 0254 852986).

Pass the end of the farm to a T-junction and take the track to the right and the gate ahead into a field. Follow the left-hand boundary to the pond and then strike off half-right, past the fence corner, and continue on the same line across a rushy field to the edge of the woods. Turn to the left along the fence and follow it into the corner by the canal. The path drops down to the canal bank and then comes back up immediately to a stile and crosses up the field to the gate by the dog-leg in the wall. Go through and ahead ten paces to a grassy track from the farm and turn to the right down the slope towards the chimney of the paper works. Cross the canal bridge.

Turn left along the towpath and follow this to the brick-built remains of a print works beside the second bridge (Finnington Bridge No 91B). Just before this bridge is a BBC booster station and the field known as Dear Bought. The story goes that a wandering mower was told by the farmer that he could have the meadow if he mowed it between sunrise and sunset of a single day. Though he succeeded, the effort killed him! Across to the right of the bridge is the tower-like house at Finnington Bar, which used to be the toll point on the turnpike road.

Go under the concrete and steel structure (1936) to steps up to the road on the right on the far side. Turn back across the bridge, taking care for traffic, and take the path to the right in 20 yards at the gate. Walk parallel to the canal to a stile at the far end of the field and then cross the next field diagonally to the right to the A675 by a small bridge at the head of a wooded clough. Go directly ahead across to the track to Brimmicroft and bear left at the T-junction and into the yard between a horse exercise yard and a barn. Cross straight over to a stile and continue ahead in the same direction, under the power line, and between hedges of cut holly. At the gate, use the stile and turn to the left along an old drove road, now well wooded and churned up by cattle underfoot when wet. This brings you out to the A674 almost opposite the Hoghton Arms.

26 Belmont
The Wright's Arms

The Belmont of today derives from a mill village developed for the workers of the dye and bleach works around 1800, beside the newly turnpiked road. This was part of a general move out from Bolton itself to sources of clean water and plenty of cheap land on which to stretch out cloth to bleach it in the sun (apparently the alternative was to send it to Holland for bleaching). The mill straddles the lane to Egerton and is still operational. It was the mill owners who renamed the village from the former Horden – a change in meaning from 'dirty valley' to 'beautiful hill'.

The interior of the Wright's Arms underwent a total refurbishment during 1993. The superb views from the rear, out across Longworth Clough and Egerton, to Turton Heights, are now complemented by a modern, light and airy interior which still chimes in well with the exterior of local sandstone. The age of the building is uncertain but it is, perhaps, of the late 19th century. Lunchtime food is served, Monday to Friday, between 12 noon and 2 pm. In the evenings, serving times are from 6 pm to 9 pm Sunday to Thursday, and to 10 pm on Friday and Saturday. Those old favourites of Lancashire lads and lasses, fish and chips with mushy peas, and steak and kidney, remain firmly on the top of the menu here. At the same time, the place has branched out into more varied cuisine. You can start with breaded mushrooms (as well as Yorkshire pudding), and try cashew nut pancakes (in addition to chicken Kiev) to follow. The vegetarian will find things like tuna pasta bake, and the lighter eater a small lamb rump steak to tempt them. Sweets and specials are chalked up each day.

Tetley and Cains ales are on draught, and also Old English cider. Drinking hours are 12 noon to 3 pm and 6 pm to 11 pm Monday to Saturday. Sunday hours are 12 noon to 10.30 pm. A non-smoking area is provided. There is a beer garden and also an outside area for the children. Dogs are not permitted in the pub.

Telephone: 0204 811296.

How to get there: On the A675 Bolton to Preston road, about ½ mile on the Bolton side of Belmont village.

Parking: Generous parking is available at the pub, which walkers are welcome to use.

Length of the walk: 3 miles. Map: OS Landranger 109 Manchester (GR 679153).

The walk takes you in a circuit around the village, touches the edge of the moors, and then returns you via the lower end of the village street.

Belmont forms a late example of a small industrial development in a rural setting. The surrounding moors are only a reason for its existence in supplying water. The grass moorland was largely denuded of its farms when the reservoirs were built (as it was then thought to be a necessary precaution against disease). Until very recently, the ridges to the west were generally inaccessible but access has been negotiated as part of the West Pennine Moors Recreation Area and the stronger walker can use paths like that signed to Winter Hill – one of the many 'in memoriam' signs put up by the Peak and Northern Footpaths Society – as a gateway to a wide circuit around the valley.

The Walk

Go to the back, right-hand, end of the car park where there is a panel missing from the fence. This is the start of the path (there is no sign) which leads diagonally across the field to the near corner of the new garden at Greenhill. Turn to the left, beside the clough, and make your way down the slope to descend shortly, but steeply, to the nearside of the dam of the Ornamental Reservoir on the Horden Brook. Cross the fence and the top of the leet, which serves the paper works downstream, and go over the dam to a footbridge across the brook. The view up valley from this point is most attractive. Climb up the

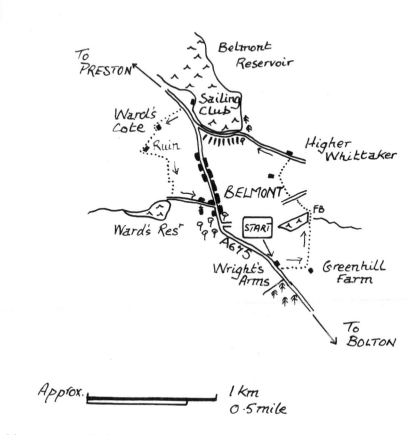

N

To
PRESTON

Belmont
Reservoir

Sailing
Club

Ward's
Cote

Ruin

Higher
Whittaker

BELMONT

FB

START

Ward's Res.

A675

Wright's
Arms

Greenhill
Farm

To
BOLTON

Approx.

1 km
0·5 mile

field to a stone stile beside a vehicle pull-in on the lane. Go left to the
second gate on the right. Turn up between the fence and wall (there
is no sign) and pass Lower Whittaker about 50 yards to the left to reach
a wicket gate. Go through this and continue up the right-hand wall to
emerge on to another lane opposite Higher Whittaker. Turn to the left
and drop slowly down to the road over Belmont Reservoir dam. Most
of the village is in view on your left as you walk down. At the far end
of the dam, follow the narrow road up to its junction with the A675
and walk to the right, along the footway, to the entrance of Bolton
Sailing Club, from which sail boats put out at weekends and on sunny
summer days. All the upper valley is open to view now and the skyline
to the left, with its peat hags, marks the divide to the Lancashire
lowlands.

Cross the main road with care and take the farm access track to the left and rise gently up to the buildings of Ward's Cote. The path goes up the right-hand of these and then round to the left. Here you will find a stile over the fence immediately on the right. Contour round into the side valley of Ward's Brook as far as the obvious ruin and cross the wooden fence on your left to it and find the two trees (an elder and a thorn) standing amongst the stone blocks. Your view has now turned through 180° to be across Bolton and as far as the Peak District.

Aim across to the nearest of the houses and take the path which runs down along the back of them to your right. Follow this round a dog-leg to go along the outside wall of the recreation ground to reach the road beside the bottom corner of Ward's Reservoir. Hang gliders and parascenders often use the steep edge on the far side of the reservoir. Turn left and walk along to the mid-Victorian (1850) St Peter's church with its steeple on the west. The site is superb, and the view to it is a well-loved addition to the landscape, especially from down beside the Ornamental Reservoir. Divert through the churchyard and come out of the bottom gate opposite the Black Dog pub. At the main road corner, cross over to the corner of Maria Square. These well-designed dwellings (1804) with their stone name plaques, have been renovated and cleaned in recent times. Some of the later buildings are on land so steep that there are two storeys to the front and four to the rear. Sadly, the red-brick police station (1900), across the road, and the adjacent modern detached houses are not of the same quality. At the same crossroads is a drinking fountain (no longer with water flowing, but with flowers in the trough) erected to celebrate Queen Victoria's Jubilee, the former Sabbath School, and an obelisk to commemorate the achievement of 'rights for all time and to perpetuity' to compensation water for the residents when Bolton took over the reservoir in 1907.

Follow the footway along the main road, past the footpath sign for Winter Hill to the right, to return to the Wright's Arms.

27 Whittlestone Head
The Crown and Thistle Inn

The formal address of the Crown and Thistle Inn is Darwen, but it is not even on the correct side of the hill for this to feel right. It, and St Mary's church, are all that you will see of the hamlet of Whittlestone Head as you pass along the Roman Road. Whittlestone Head may well signify an especially pale sandstone bed outcropping at the top of this small side valley ('whittle', in this instance, meaning white). The occupation of many of the small hamlets in the area was a combination of farming and weaving, from Tudor times down to the 19th century. Some of the older houses show the heavy stone mullions and drip stones so characteristic of northern farmhouses. Many fell on hard times but are now renovated and their barns converted into dwellings.

The pub then known as the Rose and Crown was here before 1701. It got its present name during the Jacobite Rebellion of 1745. The inn is closed on Mondays. During the rest of the week meals are served between 12 noon and 2 pm and from 7 pm to 11 pm (9 pm on Sundays). It is not the practice to print a menu but to adjust according to availability of ingredients. None the less, weekdays usually include roast chicken, fish and chips, scampi, trout and braised beef stew with dumplings. On Sundays the roast is lamb, beef or pork – and folk will

113

come a long way for it, so the quality has to be good. A variety of curries, grills, snacks, sandwiches and filled jacket potatoes is also served here.

This is a Thwaites pub and serves that brewer's ales and lagers, plus Guinness. What is different is that German, French and Italian wine and champagne are readily available. Licensing hours are 12 noon to 3 pm and 7 pm to 11 pm. One room is reserved for non-smokers and children are most welcome at any time.

Telephone: 0254 702624.

How to get there: From the A676, Bolton to Ramsbottom road, turn left along the Roman Road via Edgworth to reach the pub in 4 miles. From Darwen, take the turn for Hoddlesden from the A666 and turn right on the Roman Road at the top of the hill, a distance of about 3 miles. From this direction it is wise to slow down as you pass the church for the pub is on a hill and bend and it is all too easy to be past the car park without realising it.

Parking: The car park is immediately across the road and has limited space. Please ask at the bar before leaving your car when you go for a walk. There may be a very small amount of additional parking available by the church.

Length of the walk: 3½ miles. Map: OS Landranger 109 Manchester (GR 720198).

I suppose this is as near as one can get to what could be described as the middle of the West Pennine Moors. The circuit round the edge of Cranberry Moss includes cloughs, pasture, plantation, quarries, reservoirs and old mines, as well as open views in all directions. The Roman road runs, quite clearly, between Ribchester and Salford and long stretches across these moors are still a minor route. At the bridge (itself probably 12th century) below the pub you can see the paving flags of the Roman ford across the stream beneath it.

The Walk

Drop down to the bridge close to the pub and have a look at the Roman ford and then use the lane across the road from the pub beside the stream and along banks of heather, bilberry and fine grasses (there is no sign). In the hamlet, go between the white-painted gate-posts more or less immediately ahead, and walk round the right-hand side of The Barn and in front of its garage. Bear to the left, parallel with the railway and the clough on your left. The West Pennine railway line was built between 1845 and 1848 to link Bolton with Blackburn and still serves that function. Only Entwistle station remains open on this

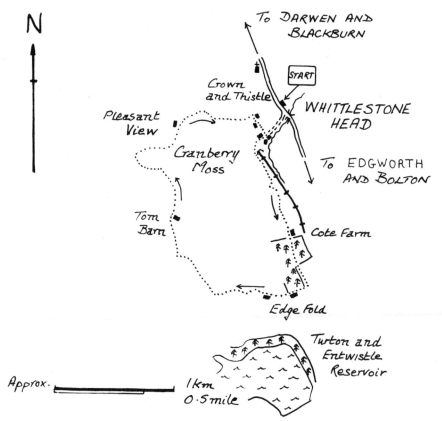

N

To DARWEN AND BLACKBURN

START

WHITTLESTONE HEAD

Crown and Thistle

Pleasant View

To EDGWORTH AND BOLTON

Cranberry Moss

Tom Barn

Cote Farm

Edge Fold

Turton and Entwistle Reservoir

Approx.   1 km
0.5 mile

side of the moor.

Quarries are visible on the left-hand slope of The Naze and the view opens up down the valley, past Edgworth (one of several 'worths' in Rossendale and the West Pennines, indicating the summer pastures of our Scandinavian ancestors) to Affetside and out across the conurbation of Greater Manchester. The track continues, with exposed sandstone rock in a side clough and gorse on the banks, to Cote Farm. Go straight in front of the house to a stile into a plantation of pine, larch and beech and walk through to the far side. The path goes ahead a further 50 yards and then turns to the right to the corner of the plantation fence and joins an old sunken track which descends slightly to Edge Fold. Pass behind the first house and then a cattery and continue on past a second house to join Edge Lane, coming up from your left. Climb up a little between old barns; Turton and Entwistle Reservoir should now be visible to the left. The reservoirs

115

serve Bolton and its satellites. The first to be built was Turton and Entwistle (1831), Wayoh then followed (1876), and Jumbles completed the sequence in the Bradshaw valley as recently as 1971.

Proceed along the track, which now swings up slightly and bears right before dropping down in a wide sweep to the left to a stile by a gate leading up to the right to the isolated building of Tom Barn. The view from the gate is across to Turton Heights, with Winter Hill beyond, and Black Hill (well named as you see it), at the northern end of Darwen Moor, more or less dead ahead. At Tom Barn, cross to the left of the building, between it and the pond, and exit on to the access road. Follow this over the crest and descend to a T-junction and bear left to a second T-junction. At this point, turn to the right and climb up past the strange concrete capping of an old mine shaft; the view down the Darwen valley, over Darwen Town, and out towards the fells of Bowland is quite stunning from here. It is no wonder that the farm you next come to is called Pleasant View.

At the farm, walk past on the right of the outbuildings and keep along the right-hand boundary of the next two fields. In the corner there are two parallel wooden fences. For no obvious reason, only the far one has a stile for the path and you will have to climb over the near one. The short stretch in between can be very wet. Once in the far field, bear right of the old brick ventilation shaft and stride over the ditch by a thorn tree (there was once a stone footbridge here) and go down to the broken wall. Bear along this to your left along a faint grassy track, with St Mary's church in sight, to eventually go between walls and reach a fenced gap. Squeeze between the end of the fence and the wall and find an old Peak and Northern Footpaths Society signpost. Turn to the right and go through the gate and between the houses right and left to return to the hamlet of Whittlestone Head beside the white-painted gates. Turn up to the left to reach the Crown and Thistle.

28 Helmshore
The White Horse

Helmshore (named from the cattle shed which, a thousand years ago, stood beside the steep cliffs above the river) has both lost and gained in recent times. The new motorway, on the far side of the valley, tends to pull both traffic and commerce away from it, whilst the very absence of the former has led to a general upgrading of the care for property which gives it a brighter look than it had a generation ago. It has the doubtful distinction of having recorded some of the highest rainfall in these parts.

The White Horse stands by the road at the southern end of the village in a fashion which suggests its builders had confidence in its future. The square-cut, flush-pointed sandstone implies a late Victorian (or perhaps, early 1900s) origin, but there is no date on it. The lengthy interior of the building is a well-polished and comfortably laid-out venue. Serving hours for food are 11.30 am to 10 pm Monday to Saturday, and 12 noon to 10 pm on Sundays. The very extensive 'Brewers Fayre' menu is on offer (see also Walk 30). With seventeen main dishes (three vegetarian), seven starters (two vegetarian) and five desserts – not to mention sandwiches, salads and snacks – it is only practical to give a suggestion of choices. I rather fancied breaded fish

117

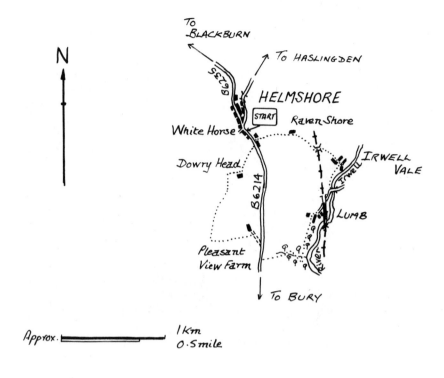

pieces with a dip to start, followed by vegetable harlequin, then a Black Forest sundae. There are daily specials in both main meals and sweets (including a tasty-looking mushroom and nut fettuccine when I was last in). Children's portions are available.

Licensed hours are 11 am to 11 pm Monday to Saturday, and 12 noon to 10.30 pm on Sundays. Boddingtons beers are served on draught, plus guest beers. A list of twelve bottled wines gives a choice to accompany a meal and three basic house wines can be ordered by the carafe or glass. A non-smoking area has been set aside and there is a beer garden. Families are most welcome, but dogs are not permitted inside the pub.

Telephone: 0706 213873.

How to get there: At the junction of the B6235, Helmshore to Blackburn road, with the B6214 from Ramsbottom and Bury via Holcombe Brook, or from Haslingden.

Parking: There is a large car park at the rear and the landlords are quite used to walkers wishing to leave their vehicles.

Length of the walk: 3 miles. Map: OS Landranger 103 Blackburn and Burnley and 109 Manchester (GR 782205).

The walk route explores the valley from its floor to the open pastures of the upper sides. On the way, the industrial past and present are visited and the surprisingly rich banks of the Irwell (the 'winding' river) and the nearby woodland are seen. The quarries visible from the route are just one small part of a massive industry which has still not ended. In the past the prize was the even-surfaced, flat-bedded 'Haslingden flags' which produced road sets, kerbs, lintels, doorsteps and many other items, as well as paving flags. Today, such operation as there is produces mainly path gravel and roadstone.

The Walk

Cross the road in front of the pub and walk up the footway to the footpath to the left on the near side of a small terrace of houses. Pass Irongate Barn on your left and proceed down the track. Across the field to the left, grazed by a mixture of Jacob sheep and donkeys, the centre of Helmshore is in view. Go between the buildings of the old farm of Raven Shore and bear right at the turn by the house on the right just beyond. The view is now to the far side of the Irwell valley and the massive quarries on the hillside of Scout Moor above Ramsbottom. The track drops between hedges of thorn, holly, elder, alder and rose, to cross a stone bridge over an old railway cutting and then goes down past the terraced houses of Milne Street to the centre of the hamlet of Irwell Vale. This tiny and still functional industrial hamlet is a Conservation Area. The Aitkens rebuilt an earlier mill here in 1826 and began the production of sailcloth. The houses, chapel and other facilities all largely date from this time.

Turn to the right between the nursery school and the Methodist chapel and follow the path round the car park and through the fields beside the river Irwell. At the wicket gate on to a lane at the next bridge you will find an 'Irwell Way' sign; turn right. The Irwell Way follows the valley from Bury to its head. From near dereliction as a result of pollution, this short section shows how quickly nature has taken back its own.

Walk under the arches of the old viaduct and into the hamlet of Lumb. Pass Lumb Grange and go half-right up the bank towards the signed 'Herons Reach Apartments'. Bear to the left round the rear of two rows of brick terraces and go ahead through the white iron gates. Take the stile, almost immediately, to the right-hand side of the fence and follow along to enter the wood, passing a couple of empty works ponds and a large shed on the left. Follow the path through the oak wood above a steep, shaley cliff dropping into the river and cross a tumbling side clough with carpets of moss and exposed beds of rock.

119

Climb up a little and then go down again to the next side stream, almost at the far edge of the wood. Turn up to the right along the stream beyond a short length of old built-up path. Cross over and make your way to the right-hand boundary wall and up the field above the wood, first to a stile over a fence, and eventually to the field gate on to the B6214 (the stile which ought to be in the fence to the left seems to have disappeared).

Turn right along the footway and pass the Second World War pill-box in the field on the left. Cross over the road to the access track for Pleasant View farm and look for the stone stile to the left beyond the bungalow. This is a difficult stile to manoeuvre. Take a line directly up the field to a point about 30 yards left of the stone hut at the top wall; here there is another rather awkward stile (alternatively, go just right of the hut to the gate). The path continues up over a hummocky field to a gate on to a stoned track between walls. Immediately across is an old well with the remains of a stone marker. The view now extends from Pendle Hill, to the north, to the Peak District to the south. Northwards also, and half-left, is the valley of Haslingden Grane and another great set of quarries on Musberry Heights.

Follow the track to the right, dropping all the while, to a T-junction close to the entrance to Dowry Head. Turn right and immediately left through the small iron gate into the field by the entrance and walk along the hedge line to the far end of the house. Turn left at right-angles down the near side of the fence at this point and follow the boundary through to rejoin the B6214 opposite the other end of the terrace of houses from which you started. Turn back left 300 yards to the White Horse.

About half a mile north of the White Horse, on the B6235, is the Museum of the Lancashire Textile Industry, which is unique in the North. Opening is in the afternoons from 1st April to the end of October and from 11 am on Sundays (telephone 0706 226459). Here it is possible to see the full process of spinning in Whitaker's Mill and the process of fulling (pounding of the cloth to tighten up the weave) in the older (1789) Higher Mill and learn – perhaps for the first time – what Hargreaves' Spinning Jenny and Arkwright's Water Frame were actually like.

Limbrick
The Black Horse

A notice on the wall inside the Black Horse suggests its history began in AD 997! Be that as it may, it certainly seems to have been the first recorded licensed house in Lancashire, having been licensed by the magistrates of Leyland Hundred for the sale of ales in 1577. The present building was also a farm 76 years ago – I happened to bump into a lady who was born and brought up in it – and the pub looks very much part of the landscape. The changes made to the inside in recent years are in no way apparent to the visitor and this up-and-down, low-ceilinged hostelry takes you back in time. Food is served at lunchtimes between 12 noon and 1.45 pm and also at weekends from 7.30 pm to 10 pm. No menu is printed so you must call to see what is currently available on the boards. The range is quite extensive and international but it is the only place I have come across where you can make a real meal of black pudding and mustard in the old Lancashire way. There would be little difficulty in persuading me to surround this with home-made soup and treacle sponge – back to the days of my youth! Sandwiches, salads and baked and filled potatoes cater for the less hungry and there is a specials board each day.

This is a Matthew Brown (Scottish & Newcastle) house with its own bitter and mild and also Theakston Best Bitter and Extra bitter. McEwan's lager, Beck's beer and Guinness on draught are other choices. Opening hours are 11 am to 11 pm (10.30 pm on Sundays). A beer garden is to the rear. Dogs are not allowed inside the premises. Telephone: 0257 264030.

How to get there: Approach from the A6 at Adlington (about 3 miles), or from Chorley turn on the road signed for Cowling and Rivington off the B6228 at the Seven Stars pub (about 2 miles). The pub stands on the hill on Long Lane.

Parking: There is a reasonably large car park across the road. As an alternative, you can make the pub the halfway point of the walk by using the very small amount of roadside parking at the head of Anglezarke Reservoir.

Length of the walk: 4 miles. Map: OS Landranger 108 Liverpool and 109 Manchester (GR 602163).

This is the western edge of the West Pennine Moors Recreation Area which covers 90 square miles and stretches east to Haslingden and from Blackburn in the north to Bolton in the south. The reservoirs (usually referred to as Rivington reservoirs – though there are eight in total in this immediate area and only two of them are actually called after that village) are a major recreational attraction with the dramatic backdrop of the Anglezarke moors and the waterside woods. The latter are especially attractive in autumn.

The walk route contrives to include pastureland, water edge, woodland and one of the lower heather-covered tops at Grey Heights – once part of a royal park on Healey Nab. At the same time it contrasts the past (these moorlands have many prehistoric sites) with the most modern of major countryside changes – the M61 motorway. Standing under the bridge by the river Yarrow at Limbrick it is hardly believable that the roar above is in any way related to the quiet scene below. 'The slope of the lime trees' seems a very credible name for this spot.

The Walk

From the pub doorway, turn right down to the bridge over the river Yarrow and go right up Back Lane, past a terraced row of houses, and under the motorway bridge. In 20 yards, part-way up the climb of the bank beyond, bear off to the right and drop back down to river level past an aqueduct piped across the river. Walk through the field by the river and cross a side stream on a small stone bridge. At the far side of the next field, move up left beside a runnel and above the beech trees and go straight up the field to a footbridge carrying a waymark arrow. Follow the right-hand hedge and in 100 yards use the gap on

122

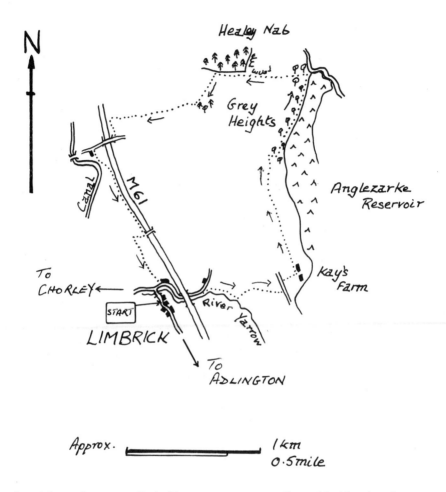

N

Healey Nab

Grey Heights

Anglezarke Reservoir

Canal

M61

To CHORLEY

START

LIMBRICK

River Yarrow

Kay's Farm

To ADLINGTON

Approx. |‖————————‖| 1 km
0.5 mile

the right and cross a ditch (there was once a stile and bridge here) to the far side of the hedge and continue on the same line to the field gate on the left. Just beyond this, and level with the farm buildings across to the right, take a stile to the left and then go over a small field to emerge on to a lane.

Turn left for 20 yards and then go right on the bridleway up the access track for Kay's Farm and Heath Fold. Just before the latter, the bridleway turns left along a track between fences – thought once to have been a Roman road. Across the reservoir to your right are the former Leicester Mill quarries, with the shoulder of Grain Pole Hill rising behind them. Follow the track along the contour towards Grey

Heights ahead and, at the start of the woods on the right, take the stile to the right by the sheep pens. Drop down the path through mixed woods of oak, sycamore, beech and holly to walk beside the reservoir wall. Someone is bound to be fishing along this stretch; I met a craftsman repairing the wall – not a frequent sight these days; across the water is the black and white water bailiff's cottage. The path reaches a lane at the head of the reservoir, where there is alternative parking.

Just before the lane, take the stepped path steeply up to your left and out of the wood. Continue straight up the field and cross over a track as you reach the edge of heather moorland and the spoil heaps of a former quarry. Go straight across and follow the clear path over the brow, worn down to the sandstone rock under foot, and over a crossing of tracks to drop a little to a fork of paths at the corner of a plantation. Use the stile on the left (*not* the bridleway signed to the right) and follow up the line of the wall to a cairn of stones on top of Grey Heights, with a view over Chorley town and beyond and to Rivington Pike and even North Wales on a clear day.

Take the path which descends to the left and pass a small pine plantation on the left and reach a crossing of paths. Go straight ahead and drop quickly, through gorse and scrub willow (muddy in parts) to cross the fields towards the M61. Over the stile at the bottom bear to the left parallel to the motorway and walk to the first bridge across it to the right. Go over the bridge and go left on the near side of the first bungalow on the left. A stile leads into a field and the path leads up between a broken wall and an old hedge line to run beside the motorway and behind the massive storage sheds of the Matthew Brown brewery until you come to a footbridge over the motorway to the left. Ignore this and turn sharp right down the field to the gap between a hedge and a fence end. Use the stile to the left and follow the line of the path through behind the cricket ground and along a scrubby lane to emerge on to Back Lane beside the terrace. Bear right and left back to the start and the Black Horse.

Great Harwood
The Gamecock

The Gamecock has a resident ghost. In the 1820s the daughter of the landlord was killed by a passing mail coach and he subsequently hanged himself. The present landlord finds the result is a resident poltergeist which causes things to move and pictures to come off the wall.

The names of the inn and the former brewery owners are carved in stone on the façade of the Gamecock (by which is meant a fighting cock, rather than a grouse). A pub has stood on this spot since the 15th century and it is the oldest in Great Harwood. It was formerly known as the Cock, or the Cock Bridge Inn (the bridge still bears the name). The present building is a pleasant blend of sandstone and black and white decorative timber. It is the halfway house between Great Harwood and Whalley and is still a very popular place to come for food and drink. Now a Whitbread house, it is another of the pubs which has adopted the 'Brewers Fayre' menu (see also Walk 28). Food service is from 11.30 am to 10 pm and from 12 noon to 10 pm on Sundays. Although standardised menus can be something of a constraint on your choice, this one is so large that its combinations readily exceed the total number of pubs in this book. I had no difficulty in fancying Cajun chicken fingers as a starter, together with a steak and mushroom pudding main course, followed by chocolate mint-chip ice-cream. Vegetarians can have crispy vegetable parcels, Mediterranean vegetable casserole, and a banana boat with cream.

Weekday licensing hours are 11 am to 11 pm, and 12 noon to 10.30 pm on Sundays. Boddingtons, Castle Eden, Marston's Pedigree and a guest beer are normally on draught. There is a no-smoking area and a beer garden to the rear. A garden area is also available for children. Please ask at the bar before bringing your dog into the pub. Telephone: 0254 883719.

How to get there: Beside the A680, Accrington to Whalley road, just south of the bridge over the river Calder.

Parking: There is plenty of parking at the pub available for your use.

Length of the walk: 5 miles; ½ mile is added for the diversion into Whalley town. Map: OS Landranger 103 Blackburn and Burnley (GR 745339).

The river is the second (or, since it is larger and longer, perhaps it is the first?) Lancashire Calder (see also Walk 7), which rises near Todmorden and enters the Ribble just below Whalley. The gap it uses between the bulk of Pendle and Whalley Nab must be a post-Ice Age channel. The walk follows the valley and then climbs over Whalley Nab before dropping back on the Great Harwood side.

The Walk
Turn towards the bridge from the pub doorway along the footway and take the path signed 'Whalley Nab' just past the cottages. Drop down the field to a stile and footbridge by some large beech trees to walk along the banks of the river Calder, where grey wagtails bob amongst the flotsam of winter floods. At the next side stream, cross the stepping stones and climb up the wooded bluff on the outside of the bend. The views downstream, through the narrow valley, are especially appealing in autumn. At the up-and-over stile by a seat continue straight on and drop steeply down a stepped path to a stone flag bridge over the Dean brook and into fields where Himalayan balsam graces the banks. The path swings up to the left, crossing an old, overgrown track lined with holly and thorn, and contours round into a small side valley. The view right is now of the bulk of Pendle Hill and through the gap to Padiham. Another stone footbridge takes you across the stream, and, almost immediately, stepping stones and a stile bring you back to the same bank. Rise gently up the field to a point opposite a stone barn up to your left and use the stile to the right

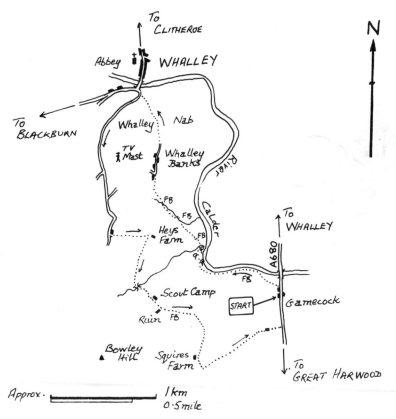

To CLITHEROE

Abbey ✝ WHALLEY

To BLACKBURN

Whalley Nab

TV Mast

Whalley Banks

River Calder

FB

FB

Heys Farm

FB

To WHALLEY

A680

FB

Scout Camp

START

Gamecock

Ruin FB

Bowley Hill

Squires Farm

To GREAT HARWOOD

N

Approx. |_____| 1 km
0·5 mile

(*not* the one ahead) to recross the stream for the third time and bear up diagonally to the right to join the old packhorse track at the right-hand corner of the field.

Turn right on the old raised footway and walk through along a short length of access track past Whalley Bank farm and join the metalled surface of Dean Lane. Dean Lane is, quite clearly, one of the old pack-horse routes, which came this way to avoid the wet valley bottom. The short section by Whalley Banks shows an excellently preserved example of the separate footway raised above the horse route below. Bear right along the lane, past several houses, until it degenerates into a track again, in about 200 yards, and follow through past the modern buildings at Three Views. Down to the right the wide meanders of the river will be plainly in view. The access track slowly bends to the left and gradually works its way down the face of Whalley Nab through what was once Nab Wood and is now entirely pasture. The wide view extends over Whalley town, up the valley to

Clitheroe and across to Longridge Fell and the fells of Bowland.

At the lane there is the opportunity to go steeply down to the bridge and cross to view the remains of the abbey and the present church, as well as the town itself. The obvious church in Whalley town is St Mary's and it is the finest 13th century church in the county; it is older than the abbey. Its woodwork is very fine, especially the seat carvings. The abbey lay to the south-west of it, beside the river. The monks arrived here in 1296 and it was dissolved by King Henry VIII's order in 1538.

Whalley town preserves the atmosphere of the past so well simply because the local worthies refused to let industry develop there in the 18th and 19th centuries – hence the mills in Billington across the Calder. The railway viaduct, to the west of the town, opened in 1850 to carry the line from Blackburn to Clitheroe.

If you wish to remain on the main walk turn up the hill to the left and walk along the lane under the beeches and pass Nabside farm on your right. Pass the TV mast on the left and ignore both Moor Lane, to the right, and the lane labelled 'Unsuitable for HGVs' to the left, to reach a new plantation of pines on top of the hill, where some of the underlying sandstone is exposed, and take in the view which opens out over Great Harwood and to Oswaldtwistle Moor, beyond Accrington. Drop down a short distance further along the lane to Moor End and take the path to the left down the rough surfaced Berry's Lane between high banks and hedges. The view is now across the Calder valley to Sabden, below Pendle.

At the bottom of the lane, before reaching the yard of Heys Farm, turn sharply to the right along what is, once again, Dean Lane. Follow this along the contour, with the pudding-shaped Bowley Hill across the Dean valley in front of you, until you drop down a partly stone setted slope to a massive stone bridge over the Dean Brook. Over the other side, climb up again, on the remains of the setted surface to a blue footpath sign (an unusual and confusing choice of colour) at the junction of tracks. Turn left and immediately go under the entrance arch of Bowley Scout Camp. The path goes immediately to the right, in front of the buildings, and to the corner of the ruined barn in the first field. Continue ahead over two stiles and drop 50 yards left to a stile in the hedge and a poor footbridge over the ditch. Turn diagonally left down to the gate in the right-hand corner and walk by the right-hand hedge to join the path below by some seats by a stile. Walk ahead past the buildings of Squires Farm to a stile to the left at the bend of the access track. Aim, at right-angles directly down the field, towards the white house along a faint track. Pass by Roger Hey and exit to the main road. Use the footway on the far side to return 250 yards to the Gamecock.